SCIENCE ENRICHMENT ACTIVITIES
for the Elementary School

Also by the Author

Arithmetic Enrichment Activities for Elementary School Children
(Parker)

A Galaxy of Word and Spelling Games for Elementary School Children
(Parker)

Language Enrichment Activities for the Elementary School
(Parker)

Treasury of Classroom Arithmetic Activities
(Parker)

Guiding the Gifted Child
(Random House)

Individualizing Instruction in the Elementary School
(Random House)

SCIENCE ENRICHMENT ACTIVITIES
for the Elementary School

Joseph Crescimbeni

Parker Publishing Company, Inc.
West Nyack, New York

Library of Congress Cataloging in Publication Data

Crescimbeni, Joseph.
  Science enrichment activities for the elementary
school.

  Includes index.
  1. Science—Study and teaching (Elementary)
2. Activity programs in education. I. Title.
LB1585.C67   372.3'5'044   80-28026
ISBN 0-13-794693-7

Printed in the United States of America

Dedication

To my son, John,
for his loyalty and support

The Value of This Book

TO THE TEACHER

Pupils see science as a subject that is challenging, interesting, and changing continuously. They also see science as a subject that helps them to answer their questions and solve some of their daily problems. Science is one of the few areas which provide them with stimulation and active understanding on a regular basis. The world of science surrounds them and they are fascinated by its basic tenets and ramifications.

Textbook science is not adequate in a world that is changing because of numerous technological advances. While the basic principles of science remain fairly static, students must rely upon other sources of information to supplement their basic instructional program. Games, puzzles, and activities based on science facts, concepts, and generalizations provide students with an enrichment atmosphere of intellectual stimulation. They enjoy doing these types of puzzles because they are short, definitive, can be completed in a short period of time, and also give them a sense of satisfaction apart from their instructional purpose.

Science enrichment activities, therefore, become a tempering medium of learning. They provide the basic reinforcement of facts, along with the challenge of surprise and mystery to enhance basic learning. Students eagerly seek to satisfy their curiosity in these types of learning challenges.

This book will help you, the daily stimulator of learning, to help the students develop a science vocabulary, acquire science facts, concepts, and generalizations, and develop science understanding through an independent series of learning activities which cover a wide spectrum of elementary school science topics.

This book will provide you with an abundance of self-motivating activities to direct the student's performance toward developing an "attitude of scientific inquiry." One of the basic purposes for the teaching of science is to develop an inquiring mind. These activities serve as a foundation for this purpose. Enrichment activities provide the students with the ability to recognize the problem, identify the problem, and gather the necessary information to solve the problem. This scientific method of learning is a basic parameter throughout this book.

Students are curious about what is going on in the world around them. Television, newspapers, magazines, and journals constantly bring to their attention new scientific happenings around the world. Such happenings may include the launching of a new communications satellite, a volcanic eruption, the discovery of new historical artifacts, or even the discovery of a lost colony of people. Children will want to know more about these things as their minds develop an attitude of inquiry. The activities in this book pursue the same objective. They give children the opportunity to test their knowledge, to research additional information, and to develop information on a higher plane of thinking and application.

The book covers all of the basic units of study found in the elementary school curriculum, including the study of the universe, the earth, the nature of matter, kinds of living things, environment and ecology, the importance of good health, the human body and how it works, safety and first aid, and phenomena and physical changes. Pupils will learn about machines and their uses in the control of the environment. They will learn basic information about weather and adaptation to it for human survival.

Use these activities at the end of a unit or to reinforce a particular learning concept or fact during the study of the unit. They can also be used independently by presenting one activity for each teaching day of the school year. The activities are flexible and designed to assist you in your regular teaching program. Moreover, all of these activities have been tested in the elementary classroom and are functional, practical exercises in learning. Children enjoy them and they help to individualize the learning process and fulfill a basic need in the child's ability and willingness to learn.

The activities can easily be reproduced and are designed specifically for this purpose. Busy teachers need to have learning activities which are accessible and applicable and this book was constructed with you, the teacher, in mind.

Teaching is an art. There must be a thorough understanding of what is to be taught, how it is to be taught, to whom it will be taught, and which materials will be used to teach it. The enrichment activities in this book are directed to this last goal, offering materials that can be expeditiously used for instructional purposes.

I hope that you and your students find these mental exercises satisfying and valuable in an informal pursuit of learning.

Joseph Crescimbeni

Contents

Chapter 8. Combined Activities **193**

Chapter 9. Review Exercises **237**

SCIENCE ENRICHMENT ACTIVITIES
for the Elementary School

LIVING THINGS

INTRODUCTION TO THE TEACHER

This section on living things stresses reading comprehension and interpretation in selected exercises for several animal classifications. Included are drill exercises on mammals, fish, reptiles, and mollusks. There is an emphasis on terms, as well as specific facts about each category.

The chapter also presents activities on alphabetization, research skills, inference, and common knowledge recall about each of the topics covered. There are also drills for perceptual skills and numerical order.

The students will demonstrate cognitive skills with these puzzles and exercises. In addition, they will develop a body of knowledge about the general classification of living things and their relationships in our environment. Anagram exercises are included to help the students develop an expansive vocabulary and build spelling skills.

The chapter is arranged so that you may start at any page. However, following the order presented here provides a continuum for proper understanding.

MAMMALS

We belong to the family of *mammals*. There are many different types of mammals, yet they are all very similar in some specific ways. Here are some specific facts about mammals:

1. All mammals breathe air with their lungs.
2. All mammals are warm-blooded. This means that their body temperature stays the same in the air or water around them. Man's body temperature is 98.6 degrees Fahrenheit.
3. Most mammals have live babies, rather than laying eggs.
4. Mammals belong to the *vertebrate* family, which means that they have backbones.
5. Most mammals have some kind of hair covering and some type of limbs in front and in back although some water mammals do not.
6. Most mammals nurse their young with fresh mother's milk.
7. Mammals have special teeth for biting and chewing their food.
8. Most mammals are fairly intelligent.

Mammals usually live on land, but there are some mammals that live in the water and they are called *water mammals*. They are sometimes called fish, but this is a mistake, because mammals breathe air and must come up to the top of the water to breathe. A fish does not need to do this. Some familiar water mammals are the whale, dolphin, porpoise, otter, seal, walrus, and manatee (sometimes called sea cow).

1. Name six land mammals:

   a. _____   d. _____
   b. _____   e. _____
   c. _____   f. _____

2. Write six specific features that most mammals have:

    a. _____

    b. _____

    c. _____

    d. _____

    e. _____

    f. _____

3. Look up the following words in your dictionary and write a definition for each one:

    a. manatee   _____

    b. walrus   _____

    c. otter   _____

    d. vertebrate _____

4. List four water mammals:

    a. _____   c. _____

    b. _____   d. _____

5. What is the largest water mammal?

_____

6. Look in a science book or encyclopedia and find out the difference between a dolphin and a porpoise:

_____

_____

7. Why do you think some people refer to a whale as a fish?

_____

_____

Connect these dots and discover this playful mammal.

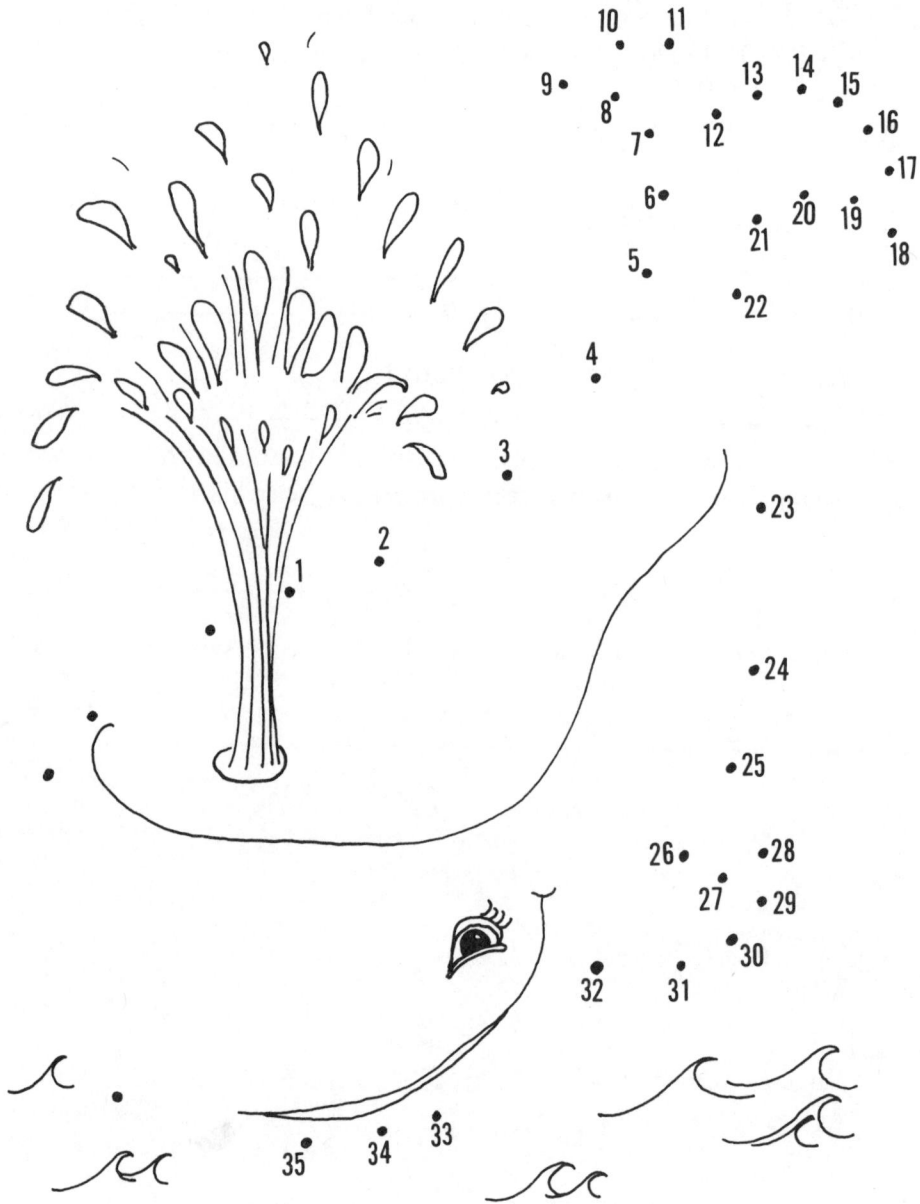

Living Things

NAME _____   DATE _____

GRADE _____   TEACHER _____

LAND ANIMALS

The names of some land animals are given below with the letters scrambled. A word clue is provided for each of the scrambled words. Look at the clue and then spell the name of the animal correctly in the space provided.

1. eder   _____   fawn
2. sorhe   _____   gallops
3. panthlee   _____   ivory
4. nukks   _____   black and white
5. claett   _____   beef
6. croupinep   _____   prickly
7. heeps   _____   woolly coat
8. yonkde   _____   stubborn
9. low   _____   hunts at night
10. oxf   _____   sly
11. geeal   _____   national symbol
12. kesan   _____   crawls
13. seiwn   _____   pork
14. olin   _____   kingly
15. terot   _____   playful
16. goanarko   _____   big jumper

ELEPHANTS

The elephant is the largest land mammal in the world. Some elephants stand 12 feet high and can weigh as much as 5 tons. Elephants eat an enormous amount of food every day, and they also love water. They are sometimes known as "hay burners" because they eat so much hay.

There are two basic types of elephants. The large African elephants have very large ears. The smaller Indian elephant is more easily trained and adaptable to work.

The elephant has four large teeth in its mouth which it uses to grind its food. Its nose is called a trunk, because it is long and like the trunk of a small tree. The trunk is really a very large muscle. Not only does the elephant use its trunk to smell, but it can also pick things up with it and use it as a very effective weapon.

The elephant has two large bones that protrude underneath its trunk. They are called *tusks*, but they are really teeth. The elephant uses them as weapons when it fights, or it uses them to dig up roots in the ground. The tusks are very valuable and are made of a substance called *ivory*. Man has hunted the elephant for its tusks. Some tusks can cost up to $5000 each. The tusks are used to make jewelry, buttons, and figurines, and they were once used to make piano keys.

The elephant is rapidly becoming extinct and is now considered one of the *endangered species*. Elephants in Africa live in a specially protected area called a *game preserve*. Elephants have been easily domesticated as work animals. They can become fine pets. Elephants can live to be 70 or 80 years old.

1. Why do you think the elephant is an unusual type of animal?

   _____

   _____

2. What are some uses of an elephant's trunk?

   a. _____
   b. _____
   c. _____

3. What is another name for a protected area where elephants live?

   _____

4. Write a definition for each of these words:

   a. ivory   _____
   b. endangered species _____
   c. tusks   _____

5. What are some uses of ivory?

   a. _____
   b. _____
   c. _____

6. What are the two main types of elephants?

   a. _____
   b. _____

7. Why would an elephant be an expensive pet?

   _____

8. Name three specific features of an elephant:

   a. _____
   b. _____
   c. _____

MAKING BIRD NAMES

Here is a list of words. Each one of these words can be changed into the name of a bird by adding the proper letter or combination of letters. Can you do this for each one of these words and name the bird that Nature has provided for us to enjoy? (Get help from a nature book, a book on birds, or an encyclopedia.)

Example: ___(pheas)___ ant

1. _____ bin
2. _____ can
3. _____ on
4. _____ awk
5. _____ ow
6. _____ row
7. _____ ken
8. _____ low
9. _____ gale
10. _____ ail
11. _____ rush
12. _____ prey
13. _____ piper
14. _____ inch
15. _____ ridge

ANIMAL ANAGRAMS

An anagram is a word from which other words can be made by rearranging the letters. Here are three separate anagrams. See how many words you can make from each one. Remember, you can use only the letters that are present in the original word.

1. *animals* (examples: a, an, aim) Make at least 20 words.

   _____
   _____
   _____
   _____

2. *hibernate* (examples: bit, tab, ate) Make 25 words.

   _____
   _____
   _____
   _____

3. *elephant* (examples: pal, ant, tan) Make 15 words.

   _____
   _____
   _____
   _____

NAME _____

DATE _____

GRADE _____

TEACHER _____

FISH

A fish is an animal that lives in the water. It is cold-blooded, which means that its body temperature changes with the temperature of the water. The temperature of the water is important for how fish feed. Fishermen must know the water temperature when they go fishing.

The fish has a backbone like a mammal, so it is also a vertebrate. Fish do not have limbs, but they have *fins* to push and swim with in the water. Fish also have *gills* for breathing. Gills can be compared with the lungs of a mammal. Most fish also have *scales* along the sides of their bodies.

Fish have nostrils which they use for smelling, just like mammals use their noses. Fish don't have ears, but they can feel vibrations in the water and they are very sensitive to these vibrations. Most fish also have very large eyes, but they do not have eyelids. Fish lay eggs and do not bear live young like mammals do. A fish rises and falls in the water by using an air bladder inside its body. This air bladder is like a balloon. The fish fills it with gas to rise up, and empties it to sink down.

The tail of a fish is very useful for steering through the water. It is like a *rudder* on a ship, which steers the ship through the water.

Fish are an important source of oil, food, and medicine.

1. Name six fish that you have seen or heard about:

   a. _____   d. _____
   b. _____   e. _____
   c. _____   f. _____

2. Write six specific features of a fish:

   a. _____
   b. _____
   c. _____
   d. _____
   e. _____
   f. _____

3. How is a fish like a mammal?

    a. _____

    b. _____

4. Look up the following words in your dictionary and write a definition for each one:

    a. fins   _____
    b. rudder   _____
    c. scales   _____
    d. gills   _____

5. What is the function of a bladder in a fish?

    _____

    _____

6. What are some uses of fish?

    _____

    _____

7. How does a fish "hear" in the water?

    _____

    _____

8. Why is water temperature important to a fish?

    _____

    _____

FISHING FOR FISH

The left-hand column is a listing of popular game fish. The right-hand column contains the same words with the letters scrambled. Unscramble the letters and write the letter next to the correct fish name.

1. bass	_____	a.	eikp
2. brim	_____	b.	nuat
3. mullet	_____	c.	lumtel
4. catfish	_____	d.	mrib
5. grouper	_____	e.	sabs
6. trout	_____	f.	sfiashil
7. flounder	_____	g.	outrt
8. pike	_____	h.	reoudlnf
9. tuna	_____	i.	reckamle
10. mackerel	_____	j.	tafsihc
11. sailfish	_____	k.	regroup
12. whiting	_____	l.	tihwing

SHARKS

A shark is a large saltwater fish. There are many different kinds of sharks, and some of them grow to be 50 feet long. The largest shark in the ocean is called a *whale shark*. Sharks, unlike other fish, do not have an *air bladder*. They must swim all of the time. Sharks can swim very fast, especially when they are going to attack other fish.

The teeth of a shark are very powerful. They are *triangular* in shape and each tooth has ragged edges like a saw. There are many teeth in a shark's mouth and a shark can easily bite another fish in half with one crunch of its powerful jaws. Sharks can also smell very well, and they can smell blood in the water a half-mile away. The shark's nostrils are spaced far apart and it can smell in many different directions. Sharks are easily attracted to things in the water by their vibrations.

Shark meat does not taste good, although some people do eat it. The skin of a shark is more important. Sharkskin is used to make wallets, shoes, belts, and handbags.

Sharks are found in all of the oceans in the world, but they stay mostly in warm waters. Sharks are hunted as "game fish." They put up a good fight when they are caught. Sharks have a healthy appetite and are known as "*predators* of the sea," which means that they hunt and eat other fish.

In recent years, the teeth of a shark have been used to make jewelry. Many communities have established "shark clubs." They hunt sharks for a hobby, and also as a means of protecting nearby beach areas.

1. Why is a shark a member of the fish family?

   _____

   _____

2. What do most other fish have that a shark does not have?

   _____

   _____

3. What are some uses of a shark?

_____

_____

4. Look up these words in your dictionary and write a definition for each one:

   a. white shark   _____

   b. predator   _____

   c. vibrations   _____

5. How long can some sharks be? _____ feet

6. Why is a shark considered a game fish?

_____

_____

7. Describe the teeth of a shark:

_____

_____

8. What are shark teeth used for?

_____

_____

9. Why are shark clubs formed?

_____

_____

10. Why is the shark considered the "predator of the sea"?

_____

_____

ANIMAL CHECKUP

Let's check up and see what facts you may know about different types of animals. Answer each question completely.

1. Name four members of the cat family:

    _____

2. Name two mammals that have tusks:

    _____

3. Name three animals that hunt at night:

    _____

4. Name a bird that loves cold weather:

    _____

5. What animal do you think is the fastest runner over
    a short distance?

    _____

6. Name two of the largest mammals in our world:

    _____

7. Name three poisonous snakes:

    _____

8. Name two animals that are known for having a high intelli-
    gence:

    _____

9. Name a small bird that makes a noise when it flies
    (it is found in America):

    _____

NAME _____

DATE _____

GRADE _____

TEACHER _____

- -

MOLLUSKS

There are many different kinds of mollusks which you may know by another name. Many people call mollusks "shellfish," because these animals live in their shells. A mollusk is an animal that has a soft body, and the shell serves to protect its soft body. A mollusk *does not* have a backbone, and therefore it belongs to the *invertebrate* family. (Remember, animals with backbones are called vertebrates.)

Snails, conches, oysters, squid, and octopus all belong to the mollusk family. Mollusks, like fish, have gills which they use to breathe oxygen from the water. The mollusk opens its mouth and takes in water, which passes over threadlike fibers called *filaments*. The filaments strain the oxygen out of the water, and the water goes back out of its body. This is the same process used by a fish.

A mollusk walks on the part of its body that is called a *foot*. The foot is at the bottom of the shell and it is used to move from one place to another. (Octopus and squid move differently.) Mollusks are used for food, ornaments, jewelry, and are the favorite souvenirs of beachcombers. The conch can be used as a horn after you punch a hole in the end of it.

The oyster, squid, and octopus are considered seafood delicacies. In America, the oyster is eaten most often.

1. List several types of mollusks:

   a. _____   c. _____
   b. _____   d. _____

2. What is the function of a filament?

   _____

   _____

3. Look up these terms and write a definition for each one:

   a. squid   _____
   b. coquina   _____
   c. conch   _____
   d. invertebrate   _____

4. List some uses of mollusks:

a. _____

b. _____

c. _____

5. Why is a mollusk often called a shellfish?

_____

_____

6. Write a good definition for the word *mollusk*:

_____

_____

7. What is the function of a gill?

_____

_____

When you connect the dots, you will find a type of mollusk.

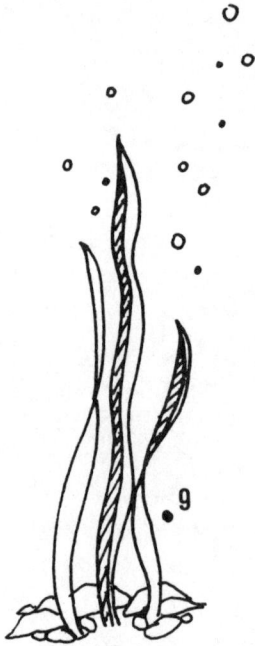

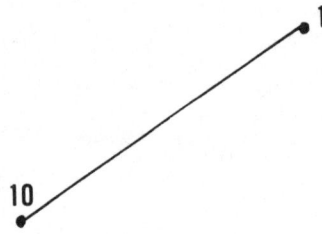

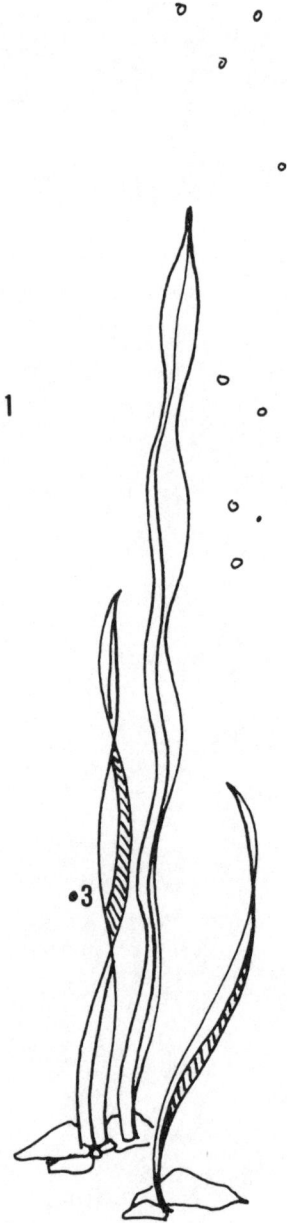

1

10

2

8 •

9

3

7 •

6

4

5

OYSTERS

An oyster is one of the most interesting types of mollusks. Not only are oysters prized as seafood delicacies, but their shells are also used for many purposes. The shiny part of an oyster's shell is called "mother-of-pearl." This part is used as a covering for knives, drums, buttons, and many other materials.

More important, the oyster also produces *pearls*. A pearl is considered to be a semiprecious stone and is used in rings, necklaces, and bracelets. Natural pearls are very rare and, therefore, also very costly.

How is a pearl formed in an oyster? The process is a simple one, but an annoying one for the oyster. A pearl is formed when a grain of sand enters the oyster's soft body. The grain of sand begins to irritate the oyster, and it *secretes* a fluid around it to relieve the irritation. When the fluid hardens, the irritation starts again. The oyster continues to secrete additional fluid until the irritation stops. This goes on for some time. The fluid has very shiny layers which make the pearl very beautiful. Most oysters that contain pearls are found in warm waters. Sometimes, a rare black pearl is found in an oyster and this is even more expensive than the white pearl. Japan has been a leading exporter of pearls, because the oysters love the warm waters that surround Japan.

An oyster has a *foot* and can move around on it. However, when the oyster grows to adulthood, it loses its foot and cannot move around. The oyster must then stay in the water right where it is, and must take water into its mouth and eat the *plankton* in it. Plankton is made up of small animals that float underneath the surface of the water. It is also one of the favorite foods of whales. Oysters stay in shallow water and are found all over the world. The natural enemy of the oyster is the starfish.

Oysters are found in large groups called *oyster beds.* Many fishermen mark off their own oyster beds in the ocean. Large nets are used to catch oysters, but sometimes they may be caught by using your hands, shovels, and baskets.

1. List some of the uses of an oyster:

    a. _____

    b. _____

    c. _____

2. How is a pearl formed in an oyster?

_____

_____

_____

3. Look up the following terms and write a definition for each one:

    a. plankton   _____

    b. starfish   _____

    c. secretes   _____

    d. irritation _____

4. What are pearls used for?

_____

_____

5. Why are black pearls more expensive than white pearls?

_____

_____

6. Who is the natural enemy of the oyster?

_____

7. What animal, besides the oyster, also likes to eat plankton?

_____

Living Things

NAME	DATE
GRADE	TEACHER

REPTILES

A reptile is a cold-blooded animal that can live on land and in the water. An animal that can live in both places is called an *amphibian*. Most reptiles live on land, but the alligator and the crocodile spend most of their time in the water. Reptiles, like mammals and fish, have backbones and are also vertebrates. Reptiles have lungs and breathe air. Most reptiles have scales and lay eggs, but some reptiles have live young.

Water reptiles include turtles, snakes, lizards, alligators, and crocodiles. The alligator and the crocodile are different from most reptiles because they can make sounds with their throats.

When reptiles swim, they close their nostrils to keep out the water. Many reptiles can stay under water for a long time. However, they must come out of water to breathe air. Reptiles like to stay in warm waters.

Most reptiles have four legs, except for snakes who wriggle through the water. Some water snakes are the black snake and the water moccasin, also called a "cottonmouth" because the inside of its mouth is white like cotton.

The alligator is the most feared reptile. It has powerful jaws and can easily crush its prey. The *hide* of an alligator is valuable and is used in making shoes, wallets, belts, handbags, briefcases, and other goods.

1. List four specific features of reptiles:

    a. _____

    b. _____

    c. _____

    d. _____

2. How is the reptile different from the fish?

_____

_____

3. Look up these words in your dictionary and write a definition for each one:

    a. amphibian   _____

    b. hide   _____

    c. sea turtle   _____

    d. crocodile   _____

4. List four kinds of reptiles:

    a. _____

    b. _____

    c. _____

    d. _____

5. Explain the difference between an alligator and a crocodile (you will need to look this up in a science book or encyclopedia):

_____

_____

6. If you had to choose a reptile as a pet, which one would you choose and why?

_____

_____

_____

FIND THE SCIENCE WORD

Rearrange the letters in each of the words below to form another word that has to do specifically with a science concept or science meaning. A clue is provided to help you think of the word.

1. sale _____ a playful ocean animal
2. mean _____ hair on a horse's neck
3. ample _____ a type of tree that gives syrup
4. battle _____ a pad of paper to write on
5. cheap _____ a type of fruit with fuzzy skin
6. deal _____ a metal that is heavy and is used in car batteries
7. diet _____ an ocean happening that occurs twice a day
8. paws _____ an insect that stings
9. heart _____ one of our nine planets
10. flier _____ a weapon used by the common soldier
11. flow _____ an animal that howls
12. shore _____ an animal that races
13. rail _____ a home for certain animals
14. melon _____ a bitter type of fruit
15. low _____ a bird that hunts at night
16. sleet _____ a metal used to make cars and wagons
17. panel _____ a vehicle used for passenger travel
18. north _____ prickly part of a flower stem

NAME _____ DATE _____

GRADE _____ TEACHER _____

TURTLES

The turtle is one of the more docile reptiles. Freshwater turtles live in ponds, lakes, rivers, and muddy streams. There is also a very large *sea turtle* which lives in the ocean. The sea turtle has been hunted for food ever since it was first discovered. Now it is becoming a rare animal and is on the endangered species list. Some turtles are as small as a quarter, while the sea turtle has been known to be over 4 feet long and weigh over 450 pounds.

One of the more common freshwater turtles is the *snapping turtle*. A snapping turtle gets its name from its very powerful jaws, which can break a pencil easily with just one snap. Some turtles bite and hold on, and this too can be very painful. The snapping turtle is a very slow swimmer and lives in muddy waters. Turtles have strong claws on their feet which they use to hold and tear their food.

The green sea turtle spends most of its time in the water. Its shell is very hard and, when on land, it must lift it off the ground in order to breathe. The sea turtle has a healthy appetite and eats quite a bit of food each day. It is very much in demand as a seafood delicacy. Turtle soup is also made from it.

Turtles *hibernate* in cold weather, although some turtles have been seen and caught swimming under ice. When a turtle hibernates, its whole body process slows down and it can go for a long time without food or water.

The turtle shell has long been used for making jewelry, eyeglass frames, combs, and other items. Baby turtles have also been a popular pet for children. However, some baby turtles have been known to carry a disease that can be harmful to people.

1. Why has the sea turtle been hunted?

   _____
   _____

2. How large can turtles be?

   _____

3. Why can some baby turtles become harmful pets?

_____

_____

4. Why is a turtle an amphibian?

_____

_____

5. Write a definition for each of the following terms:

    a. hibernation   _____

    b. tortoise   _____

    c. box turtle   _____

6. What are turtle shells used for?

    a. _____

    b. _____

    c. _____

7. How does a snapping turtle get its name?

_____

_____

8. Where are turtles found?

_____

_____

NAME _____

DATE _____

GRADE _____

TEACHER _____

Discover this reptile by connecting the dots.

41
2
3
4
1
40 42
5
39
6
34 35 36
37
33 38
32
7
31 29
8
30 9 11
10
28 12
27
25 16
24 26 17 13
23 18 15 14
22 20 19
21

Living Things

- -

UNUSUAL ANIMALS

Many animals look odd and unusual. Look up in your science book or an encyclopedia some interesting information about each of these animals:

1. armadillo

_____

2. anteater

_____

3. aardvark

_____

4. koala bear

_____

5. panda

_____

6. porcupine

_____

7. flamingo

_____

8. kangaroo

_____

9. kiwi

_____

10. kookaburra

_____

LIVING THINGS MYSTERY PUZZLE

Read each clue and unscramble the letters to form a correct word.
When you are finished, spell another word from the letters in the circles.

1. Arctic Ocean mammal   A W L R S U

2. large water areas   C O N A E S

3. sound waves   S T I B A R V N O I

4. live in a shell   S L A M C

5. spotted cat   D R A P E L O

6. cold-blooded   P I L E T E R

7. precious gems   S L E A R P

Circled word is _____ .

LIVING THINGS ALPHABETIZED WORDS

Write one word that begins with each of the letters listed below. The words must all be related to living things.

A *animals* _____

B _____

C _____

D _____

E _____

F _____

G _____

H _____

J _____

L _____

M _____

N _____

O _____

P _____

R _____

S _____

T _____

W _____

Z _____

LIVING THINGS WORD FUN

This interesting word search contains the names of many living things. Can you successfully find all of the terms listed below?

```
S E K N O D G A N T B L
R L R Q O R I S A M H H
E A A J H I L E I O S I
P H H M B B L E B L I B
T W S D M I S L I L F E
I A N U T A S C H U L R
L O O P A B M A P S I N
E L E P H A N T M K A A
J R E T S Y O F A W S T
F I N S W R A G U O C E
```

ant	sailfish	eel	mollusk
fins	gills	cat	elephant
shark	whale	mammals	amphibian
bird	cougar	lion	tuna
hibernate	reptile	oyster	

LIVING THINGS SCRAMBLED TERMS

Each of the terms below has already appeared in this chapter. A very brief definition has been given to help you determine the correct word.

1. kasrh _____ ocean predator
2. lkumlos _____ shellfish
3. durerd _____ steer by
4. rlutet _____ amphibian
5. snif _____ part of a fish
6. bitrehnea _____ period of sleep
7. ammsmal _____ breathe air
8. klantopn _____ whale food
9. doerpatr _____ a hunter
10. rapwosr _____ a little brown bird
11. ptehalne _____ large land mammal
12. wol _____ night hunter
13. lgisl _____ fish breathers
14. ysorte _____ tasty shellfish
15. piltree _____ cold-blooded
16. poledar _____ spotted
17. pbaimnhia _____ land and water
18. lacsse _____ fish covering

THE HUMAN BODY

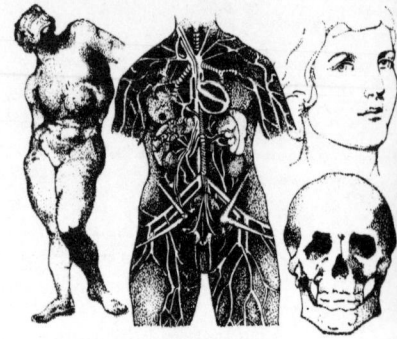

INTRODUCTION TO THE TEACHER

There are many important topics in this chapter for the elementary student to learn and understand. Major subjects for reading comprehension and understanding include the circulatory system, the digestive system, the muscular system, the nervous system, the respiratory system, and the skeletal system. Each of these sections emphasizes common facts and reading interpretation skills.

In addition, the five senses, drugs and narcotics, and first aid are also presented as basic sections of study. Alphabetization skills and research tasks are also included. Anagram practice is presented for expansion of knowledge.

Simple games are presented for reinforcement of basic facts, and inferences are included for developing the reasoning process. The material is presented at a basic level for elementary students, and they should experience very little difficulty in mastering it.

In scope, these exercises may go beyond those presented in the elementary science textbook. However, because the human body is such an interesting and important area of study, the students will enjoy tackling the tasks in this chapter.

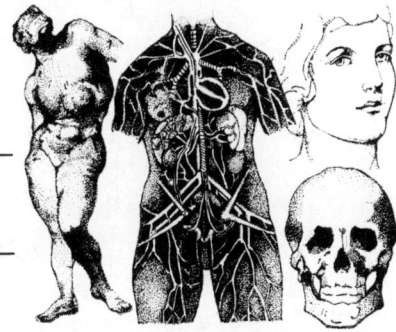

THE CIRCULATORY SYSTEM

The blood in our bodies is circulated over and over again by a large pump called the *heart*. Basically, the heart is a muscle, and as it contracts and expands it pumps the blood through veins and arteries to various parts of the body. We refer to the heart, the blood, and the blood vessels as the circulatory system because it circulates over and over throughout the body.

The blood *absorbs* the oxygen we breathe from the air and delivers it to the blood vessels and cells. It takes away carbon dioxide, which we exhale, because carbon dioxide is an impurity.

The clear, liquid part of the blood is called *plasma*. The plasma is one-tenth food, which it carries to the cells, and nine-tenths is water.

There are millions of tiny *cells* in our bodies. The cells need food and oxygen at all times or they will die. The paths which the blood takes to reach these cells are called *blood vessels*. The largest of the three blood vessels is called the *artery*. The artery carries the blood *away* from the heart. The *vein* is another blood vessel, and it carries the blood back to the heart after the oxygen has been used. The smallest blood vessels are called *capillaries*, and these reach out into each of the cells, branching like the twigs of a tree.

1. What is the function of the heart?

   _____

   _____

2. What can the heart be compared to?

   _____

   _____

3. List three types of blood vessels:

   a. _____

   b. _____

   c. _____

4. Look up these words in your dictionary and write a definition for each one:

vein   _____

artery   _____

circulation   _____

carbon dioxide   _____

5. Explain what plasma is:

_____

_____

6. What is the function of the vein?

_____

_____

7. What is the function of the artery?

_____

_____

8. Alphabetize these words correctly, using numbers 1-10.

_____ vein   _____ carbon dioxide

_____ blood   _____ oxygen

_____ heart   _____ circulation

_____ muscle   _____ artery

_____ capillary   _____ plasma

9. What is meant by *impurity*?

_____

_____

10. What is the largest blood vessel called?

_____

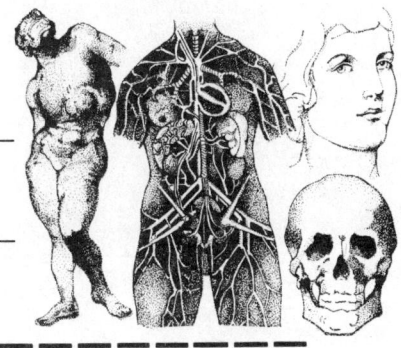

Connect the dots and discover this important human body organ.

1 •
2 •

3 •

4 •

5 •

6 •

7 •

8 •

9 •

10 •   11 •   12 •   13 •

18 •

17 •

16 •

15 •

14 •

The Human Body

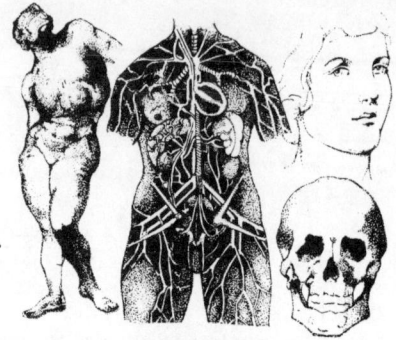

BODY PARTS

The words described by each definition below also name parts of the human body. Study the definition carefully and then write the words that fit on the blank spaces.

1. a student _____
2. a place of worship _____
3. type of tree which bears dates _____
4. name for a baby cow _____
5. part of a tree _____
6. metal used to fasten two pieces of wood _____
7. part of a shoe _____
8. name for weapons of war _____
9. middle of a hurricane _____
10. cutting edge of a saw _____
11. sounds like "knows" _____
12. sounds like "hare" _____
13. musical instrument that you beat _____
14. cut made by a whip _____

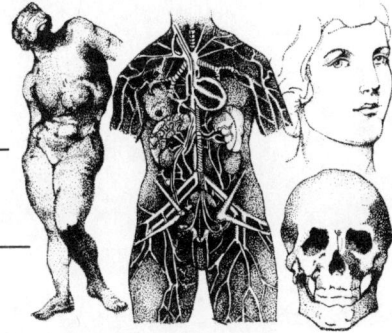

THE DIGESTIVE SYSTEM

The digestive system consists of the mouth, the stomach, and the small intestine. The mouth takes in the food, where it is broken into small pieces by the teeth. Liquid in the mouth, called *saliva*, helps to soften the food before it is swallowed. Saliva also contains a chemical called an enzyme, which changes the food into another form such as sugar, starch, or acid.

The food leaves the mouth and goes into the *stomach*. There the food is mixed with another enzyme called *gastric juice*. This juice breaks down the food and changes it some more before it goes into the blood. The stomach juices also help kill any germs that may be in the food.

The small intestine does most of the *digestion* of the food you eat. The small intestine is about 18-20 feet long in an adult. The intestine adds more juices or enzymes to the food so that the parts are broken down into very small pieces which pass into the blood. The blood then takes over and passes the food to all parts of the body.

Other organs also help in digestion. They are the liver, the gallbladder, and the pancreas. The liver and gallbladder produce a juice called *bile*, which helps digest fat in foods. The pancreas produces juices to help digest the food in the small intestine.

1. Look up these words in your dictionary and write a definition for each one:

   pancreas   _____
   bile   _____
   gastric juice _____

2. Name the three parts of the digestive system:

   _____
   _____

The Human Body   51

3. What is the function of the small intestine?

_____

_____

4. What is the function of saliva?

_____

_____

5. Alphabetize these words, using numbers 1–8:

_____ gastric juice   _____ stomach
_____ digestion   _____ bile
_____ saliva   _____ pancreas
_____ liver   _____ mouth

6. What is the function of the mouth in digestion?

_____

_____

7. How long is the small intestine?

_____

8. What is an enzyme?

_____

_____

9. How does food get from the stomach into other parts of the body?

_____

_____

10. What is the function of the liver in digestion?

_____

_____

- -

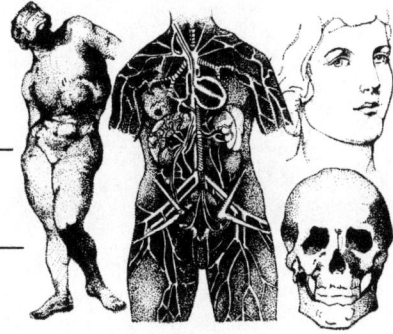

REARRANGE THE LETTERS

Rearrange each of the letters below to form the name of a body part that you may know about and recognize.

1. sebon   _____
2. seey   _____
3. ram   _____
4. wobel   _____
5. raibn   _____
6. houmt   _____
7. nive   _____
8. earth   _____
9. steo   _____
10. sear   _____
11. enso   _____
12. hetet   _____
13. twirs   _____
14. sliton   _____
15. shect   _____

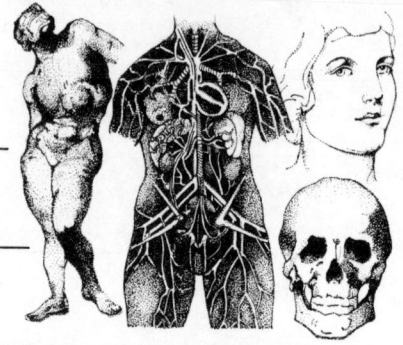

THE MUSCULAR SYSTEM

There are over 600 muscles in your body. A muscle's main function is to *contract* and *expand* so that body parts can be moved. We learned that a heart is a muscle as it contracts and expands many times. We call this movement a *heartbeat*.

There are three different kinds of muscles. One type moves the bones of the body. The upper arm muscle moves your arm and is called a *bicep*. Muscles are hooked to the bones so that the bones can move. The muscles are attached to the bones by large strings of tissue called *tendons*. A tendon can be stretched or torn and this causes much pain.

A second type of muscle is called a *smooth muscle*, and these are found in the walls of many body organs. Smooth muscles in the stomach make it contract and expand as it digests food. Smooth muscles are called *involuntary* muscles because they move automatically. *Voluntary* muscles, the ones you can control, are used when you walk, move your arms, or perform any movement.

A third type of muscle is the *heart muscle*. The heart muscle pumps blood through your heart and makes your heart beat. The heart muscle is also an involuntary muscle.

A *ligament* is not a muscle, but it is a type of strong tissue. The function of the ligament is to attach bones to bones. Ligaments can be strained and torn and when this happens they cause much pain.

1. What is the function of a muscle?

   _____

   _____

2. What attaches a muscle to a bone?

   _____

3. How many types of muscles do you have in your body?

   _____

4. Look up these words in your dictionary and write a definition for each one:

heartbeat   _____

involuntary   _____

tendon   _____

tissue   _____

5. Why is the heart a muscle?

_____

_____

6. What is the function of a ligament?

_____

_____

7. Alphabetize these words, using numbers 1-8:

_____ tendon   _____ ligament

_____ smooth muscle   _____ muscular

_____ muscle   _____ heart muscle

_____ bicep   _____ strained

8. Explain the difference between a *voluntary* muscle and an *involuntary* muscle:

_____

_____

9. List the three types of muscles:

_____

_____

10. List some involuntary types of muscles:

_____

_____

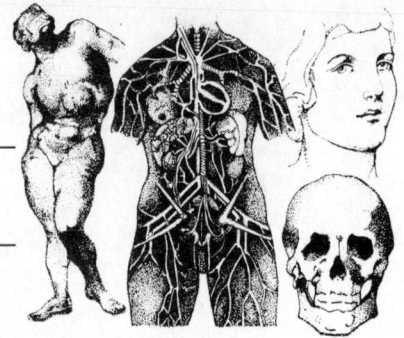

THE NERVOUS SYSTEM

The central nervous system in the human body consists of the brain, the spinal cord, and nerves. The function of the nervous system is to send and receive messages throughout the body. There are millions of nerve cells in all parts of the body and they connect directly to the brain and to the spinal cord.

There are two types of nervous systems. The *involuntary* nervous system works directly with the brain. If you touch a hot object, the nerves send the message to the brain and it automatically responds by sending you a message to withdraw your hand. The involuntary nervous system works very fast. The *voluntary* nervous system takes longer. For instance, you may want to plan out your homework, or build something in your garage. The voluntary nervous system is one which you can control.

Nervous systems depend on sense organs. A bright light may make you unable to see temporarily. You automatically shut your eyes. Or you may smell a bad odor which may cause you to cover your nose. These reactions are called *reflexes*. A reflex is a fast response to something. The nerves that respond to senses are properly called *sensory* nerves. Sensory nerves control seeing, touching, hearing, smelling, and tasting.

The nerve cells that travel from the brain to move parts of the body are called *motor* nerves. In this case, motor means to move. The motor cells tell the muscles when to move, thereby moving your bones to do something.

1. List the three parts of the central nervous system:

   _____

   _____

2. What does a motor nerve do?

   _____

   _____

3. Define a reflex:

_____

_____

4. Name four reflex actions:

_____

_____

5. Define these terms carefully by using your dictionary:

spinal cord   _____
message   _____
sensory   _____
motor (relating to health) _____

6. What is the function of a *sensory* nerve?

_____

_____

7. Alphabetize these words, using numbers 1-8:

_____ message   _____ sensory
_____ motor   _____ spinal cord
_____ memory   _____ voluntary
_____ brain   _____ reflex

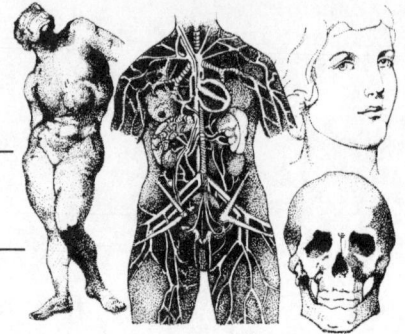

NAMING BODY PARTS

1. List eight parts of the body that have only *three* letters in their names:

   a. _____   e. _____
   b. _____   f. _____
   c. _____   g. _____
   d. _____   h. _____

2. List seven different parts of the body that have *four* letters in their names:

   a. _____   e. _____
   b. _____   f. _____
   c. _____   g. _____
   d. _____

3. List four parts of the body that have *five* letters in their names:

   a. _____   c. _____
   b. _____   d. _____

4. List three parts of the body that have *six* letters in their names:

   a. _____
   b. _____
   c. _____

5. List two parts of the body that have *seven* letters in their names.

   a. _____   b. _____

6. Write a sentence for each of these terms:

   a. brain _____

   b. ankle _____

   c. injury _____

The Human Body

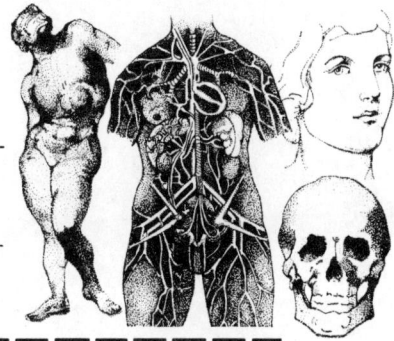

THE RESPIRATORY SYSTEM

The process of breathing, taking in fresh air and exhaling air that is impure, is called *respiration*. The nose, mouth, and lungs are important parts of the respiratory system. When we breathe, we *inhale* air which contains oxygen which is used in our blood system. When we breathe out, we exhale air containing impurities such as carbon dioxide. Carbon dioxide, like oxygen, is a gas. This gas is produced from the oxygen we breathe in after all of the food is taken out. Carbon dioxide is produced by the *cells*.

When you breathe air in through your nose or mouth, it goes down a tube called the *trachea*. The trachea extends down through your throat and then divides into two other tubes, one going to each lung. As you breathe, the air goes into the trachea and then into each tube to the lungs. The lungs contain tiny *air sacs* which are surrounded by blood vessels. The air goes out of the air sacs into the blood vessels. The blood circulates the air to all of the cells in the body. We breathe about 18 times a minute.

The function of the nose is to warm the air as it passes into the trachea. The nose also contains tiny hairs that help to *purify* or clean the air as it passes through.

Any damage to the nose can cause a rupture of the blood vessels which produces a *nosebleed*. Impurities which get past the nose and into the trachea and the lungs can cause an infection. One type of infection of the lungs is called *tuberculosis* and is a very serious disease.

1. What is the function of the nose in the respiratory system?

_____

_____

2. What three parts form the respiratory system?

_____

_____

3. Explain what is meant by *inhale* and *exhale*:

_____

_____

4. What is the trachea?

_____

_____

5. Look up these words in your dictionary and write a definition for each one:

    tuberculosis   _____

    cell   _____

    purify   _____

    nosebleed   _____

6. What is carbon dioxide?

_____

_____

7. Alphabetize these words, using numbers 1-10:

_____ exhale		_____ purify
_____ respiration		_____ tuberculosis
_____ breathing		_____ trachea
_____ lungs		_____ inhale
_____ infection		_____ air sacs

8. What is an impurity?

_____

_____

9. What is a nosebleed?

_____

_____

10. How many breaths do we take a minute?

_____

       The Human Body

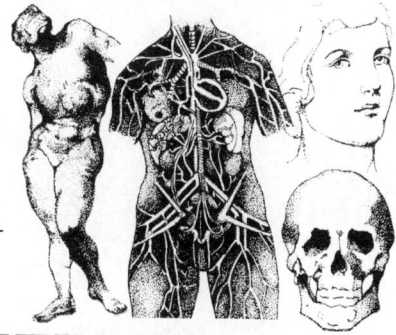

THE SKELETAL SYSTEM

All the bones in the body together are called the *skeleton*. A skeleton is an outline or framework of a particular structure. Our body's structure is called the *skeletal system*.

The skeleton allows us to stand up. It gives us our basic body shape. It determines how tall or short we may be. The skeleton also protects parts of the body from injury. The skull or *cranium* protects the brain. The chest bones protect the heart and lungs. The backbone protects the *spinal cord*.

There are over 200 bones in our skeletal system. Not only does the skeletal system contain bones, but it also contains *cartilage*, which is very strong and bends but is not quite as hard as a bone. Cartilage helps the bones move easily, and it is found in the joints, between the ribs, and in the backbone.

Bones contain blood vessels and *nerves*. The food in the bone is called *marrow*, and it is the soft part of the bone. When a bone is broken, the food in the bone helps to heal it. Bones always heal from the inside out. A break in a bone is called a *fracture*. One break in a bone is called a *simple fracture*. If you break a bone in more than one place it is called a *multiple fracture*. If the broken bone pierces through the skin, it is called a *compound fracture*.

1. What is the function of the skeleton?

   _____

   _____

2. What does a bone contain?

   _____

   _____

3. How many bones are there in the body?

   _____

4. Look up these words in a dictionary and write a definition for each one:

spinal cord   _____
cartilage   _____
fracture   _____
skull   _____

5. What large bone protects the brain?

_____

6. What is the function of cartilage?

_____

_____

7. Explain the difference between *simple, multiple,* and *compound* fractures:

_____

_____

8. Alphabetize these words, using numbers 1–8.

_____ cartilage   _____ marrow
_____ cranium   _____ nerves
_____ skeleton   _____ food
_____ skeletal   _____ fracture

9. How do bones heal?

_____

_____

10. Where is cartilage found?

_____

11. Look in an encyclopedia or science book and find a picture of a skeleton. Write the names of the bones that may be listed there on a piece of paper and learn these names.

               The Human Body

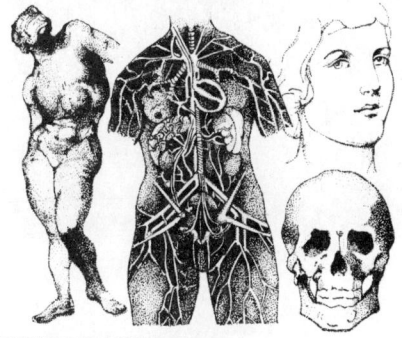

UNDERSTANDING BONES

Match the number of the bone with the word that identifies it in this list:

_____ phalanges
_____ cranium
_____ clavicle
_____ patella
_____ fibula
_____ tibia
_____ femur
_____ ulna
_____ radius
_____ humerus
_____ mandible
_____ sternum
_____ tarsals

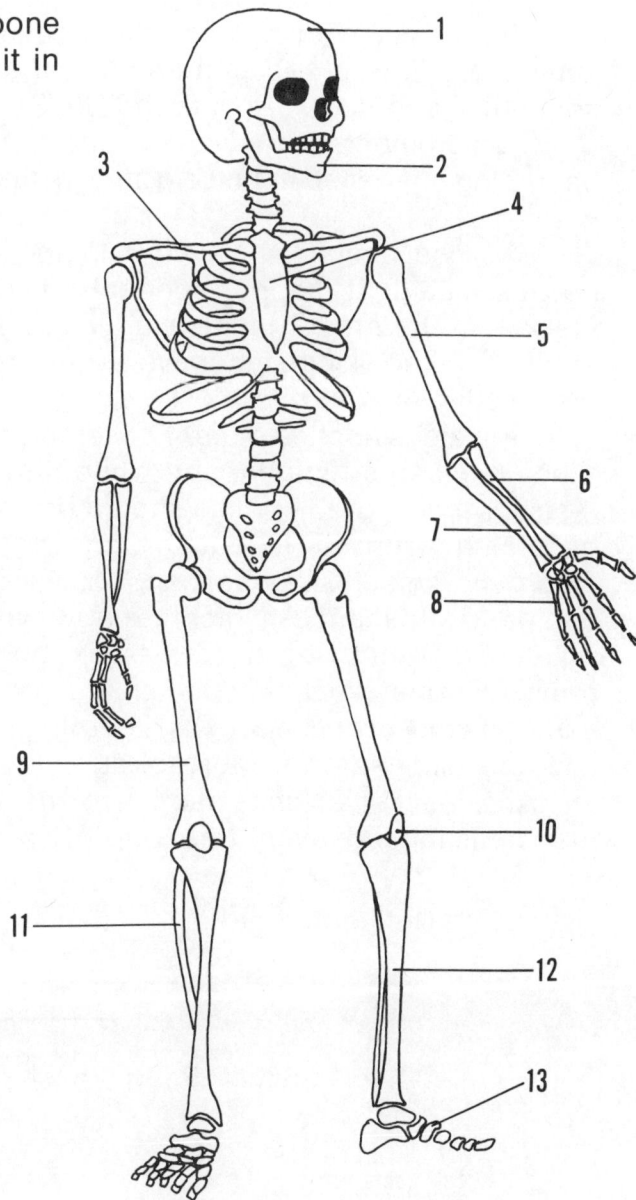

Can you memorize the names of these bones?

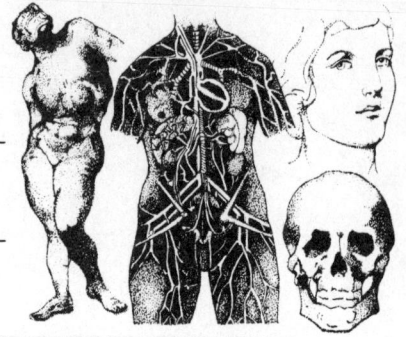

FIRST AID

First aid is the help you give immediately to a person who is injured in some way. First aid is something that every boy and girl should know something about. Boy Scouts and Girl Scouts must learn first aid as part of their requirements for advancement. Lately, more and more people are becoming interested in first aid and are taking courses to learn more about it.

Because people are always in the company of other people, and because accidents happen suddenly, it is important to know how to apply first aid in the proper medical situation. First aid is easy to learn and to apply. The knowledge you have about first aid may save a person's life. It may also save your own.

First aid is applied or *administered* only as a temporary form of relief. When accidents happen, and while first aid is being applied, a doctor, rescue service, or the police should be called. More and more people are becoming licensed to administer first aid. These people are called emergency medical technicians, or EMTs. These people ride specially equipped ambulances which are now part of almost every community.

A person studying first aid learns about applying tourniquets, locating pressure points, making splints, and keeping a person comfortable until expert medical service arrives. Learning about poisons, poisonous plants and animals, and artificial respiration is also important.

Accidents of all kinds happen all the time. Knowing how to administer first aid is indeed a very fine form of community service.

1. Define first aid:

   _____

   _____

2. What is the first thing you should do after starting to give first aid?

   _____

   _____

3. What is an EMT?

_____

_____

4. What are some of the things you will learn if you study first aid?

a. _____

b. _____

c. _____

d. _____

5. Write a definition for the word *administered*:

_____

_____

6. How many words can you make from the phrase
F I R S T   A I D?

_____

_____

_____

7. Why is it important to know first aid?

_____

_____

_____

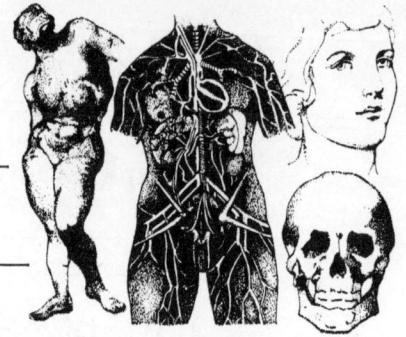

THE MEDICINE CHEST

Your medicine chest may contain some of the following well-known name brands of medical helpers. Can you find all of them in this word search puzzle?

```
B F E P A T E V I S E H D A L
S S P E R O X I D E S V I A A
P A M P E N E O T R E A M S A
L A L U O M N I N M N L P C I
A L O V T I I N E I I I E O S
C K R I E L Z T M R R U P R E
Y A L T O T A M I I D M T B N
D S A A B O R E N P E N O I G
Y E N M A W O N I M C O B C A
L L O I N W H T L E X I I A M
I T C N D G T R E S E T S C F
N Z E S A N I C A N A O M I O
A E S U I M U I R B I L O D K
U R Z A D N E D I R O D L O L
O E K A O P E C T A T E O P I
E B R O M O S E L T Z E R I M
```

Ointment
Anacin
Iodine
Tums
Vitamins
Pepto Bismol
Excedrin
Liniment
Gauze
Kaopectate
Empirim
Bromo Seltzer
Alka Seltzer
Darvon
Band Aid
Aspirin
Lotion
Milk of Magnesia
Peroxide
Thorazine
Adhesive Tape
Ascorbic Acid

The Human Body

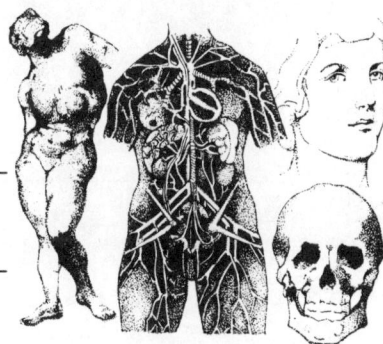

THE FIVE SENSES

The five senses are very important to the daily functioning of the body. The five senses include seeing, hearing, tasting, touching, and smelling. The senses are controlled by the brain and the nervous system. Each sense operates in a particular part of the brain. Any injury to the brain may cause an injury to the operation of a particular sense. The brain is divided into two parts, or *hemispheres*. The right side of the brain controls the left side of the body, and the left side of the brain controls the right side of the body. This may seem strange to you but that is the way it works.

The body is like a fine-tuned machine. An injury to any part of the system will slow you down. An injury to any of the senses will also slow you down. It is important, therefore, that the human body be kept in excellent condition by proper eating and well-balanced meals, by exercise, and by cleanliness.

1. List the five senses:

   _____

   _____

2. Define *hemisphere:*

   _____

   _____

3. Why is proper care of the body important?

   _____

   _____

4. Why is the human body compared to a machine?

   _____

   _____

5. What part of the brain controls the left side of the body?

   _____

   The right side of the body?

   _____

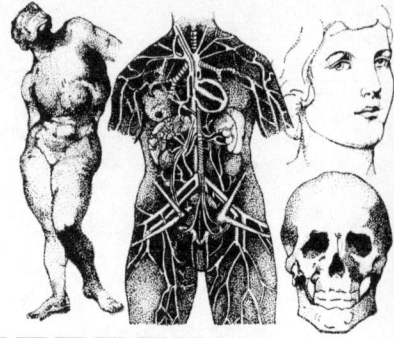

THE SENSE OF SIGHT

You use your eyes all the time. Every waking moment, your eyes are in constant use. Therefore, they should be protected and cared for at all times. Without your sense of sight, many things you do would be limited. Too often, we take our eyes for granted. They are delicate cameras that let us appreciate the world and what we do every moment of the day.

Your eyes are protected by *lashes* and the *eyelid*. The lashes keep dirt, dust, and small particles from getting into the eye. Tears form when an object gets into the eyes and help to wash the object out and reduce *irritation*. The *lens* of the eye is where the light passes through so that you can see. Any injury to the lens can be serious because it may cause a scratch that will not allow you to see properly.

The colored part of your eye is called the *iris*. The color varies in human beings and is determined by the genes of your parents. This is called *heredity*. Some people have brown irises, or blue irises, or green irises, or different shades of these colors. The black center of the eye is called the *pupil*. The pupil controls the amount of light that enters the eye. When you see something bright, the pupil gets smaller, or *contracts*. When you need more light, the pupil gets bigger, or *expands*. The eye is enclosed in the part of your skull called the *socket*. The socket helps to protect your eye against injury.

The eye is connected to the socket by six little muscles. These muscles help to move the eye. The main nerve between the eye and the brain is called the *optic nerve*. The objects you see are transmitted by this optic nerve to the brain for identification. The fluid inside the eye keeps the eye round in shape.

1. What is the function of the *pupil*?

_____

_____

2. What is the function of the *optic nerve*?

_____

_____

3. List the parts of the eye:

_____

_____

4. What function do the eye muscles play?

_____

_____

5. What is the function of the *lens?*

_____

_____

6. Alphabetize these terms, using numbers 1-12:

_____	iris	_____	tear
_____	socket	_____	heredity
_____	irritation	_____	pupil
_____	eyes	_____	lash
_____	lens	_____	eyelid
_____	fluid	_____	sight

7. Define these terms:

heredity _____

irritation _____

contract _____

8. What is the function of the *iris?*

_____

_____

9. Why should the eye be protected at all times?

_____

_____

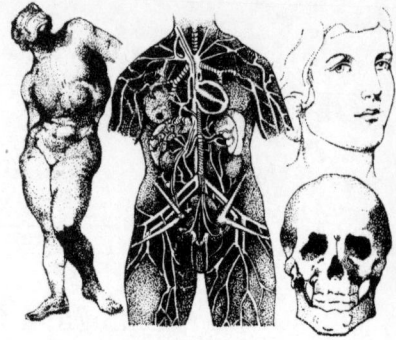

THE SENSE OF HEARING

Hearing is a very important sense. If you don't have good hearing, you cannot hear the proper sounds, and that will affect your speech. Children learn to speak by imitating what they hear. So, if you hear the wrong sound, you will say the wrong sound.

The outside part of the ear acts like an *antenna*. This antenna catches the sound and sends it to a tube inside the ear which is covered by a small piece of skin that is stretched over the opening. This is called the *eardrum*. The sounds you hear, or *vibrations,* hit the eardrum and are transferred to a liquid in the inner ear. This liquid is full of nerves, sensory nerves, which *transmit* the vibrations to the brain. Then the sound is heard.

The ear is a sensitive organ. It is protected by small hairs, like the ones in the nose, which catch germs. The ear also makes wax, which catches dust and other types of germs. This protects the inner ear, where the liquid and eardrum are located. Loud sounds, however, can break or *rupture* the eardrum. Putting pointed objects into the ear (like a pencil or a toothpick) can also rupture your eardrum. Most doctors recommend that you don't put anything into your ear that is smaller than your little finger. A ruptured eardrum causes a *hearing loss.*

Ears are also important because they give us danger signals. A toot of a horn warns you of possible danger. Because the ear is a sensitive organ, it should be washed and kept clean at all times. Remember, we appreciate a lot of what we see because we can also hear.

1. List the various parts of the ear:

   _____

   _____

2. What is the function of the outside part of the ear?

   _____

   _____

3. What is the function of the hairs and wax in the ears?

_____

_____

4. Define the following terms:

    rupture   _____

    hearing loss   _____

    vibrations   _____

    antenna   _____

    transmit   _____

5. Describe briefly how we hear:

_____

_____

6. How is hearing related to talking?

_____

_____

7. Alphabetize these terms, using numbers 1-8:

    _____ antenna   _____ hearing loss

    _____ rupture   _____ wax

    _____ eardrum   _____ inner ear

    _____ vibrations   _____ ears

8. Why should you keep objects out of your ears?

_____

_____

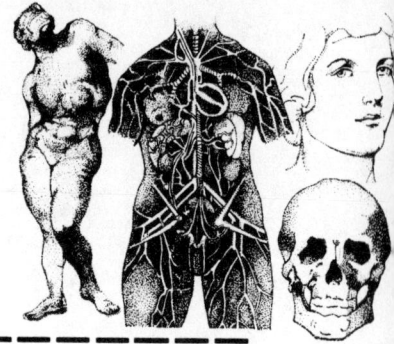

THE SENSE OF TASTE

The tongue controls the sense of taste. However, taste must also involve the sense of smell. Both the tongue and the nose control the taste of food. If your nose is clogged because of a cold, it is difficult for you to taste your food properly because you cannot smell the food properly.

There are four kinds of nerve cells found in the tongue, and these provide four separate kinds of taste: sweet, bitter, sour, and salty. The tip of the tongue tastes the sweet things. Next to that is the part that tastes sour things. Then comes the part that tastes salty things, and the back part of the tongue near the throat tastes bitter things. It is possible for different people to taste the same thing differently.

Any illness, soreness, or infection of the mouth and tongue is not only painful but also slows down your tasting process. We sometimes refer to the tasting areas of the tongue as *taste buds*, although you now know that they are really taste nerve cells. People who like fancy and exotic types of foods rely upon their taste buds all the time.

1. How many tastes can the tongue distinguish? Name them.

   _____

   _____

2. How do the tongue and nose work together to regulate taste?

   _____

   _____

3. List below five things that are salty, sour, bitter, and sweet:

	salty	sour	bitter	sweet
a.	_____	_____	_____	_____
b.	_____	_____	_____	_____
c.	_____	_____	_____	_____
d.	_____	_____	_____	_____
e.	_____	_____	_____	_____

4. What is a taste bud?

_____

_____

5. Why is the sense of taste important?

_____

_____

6. Explain which part of the tongue is responsible for which type of taste:

_____

_____

7. If someone blindfolded you so that you could not see an object you were tasting, and your nose was pinched so that you could not smell it, how accurate do you think your tasting process would be?

_____

_____

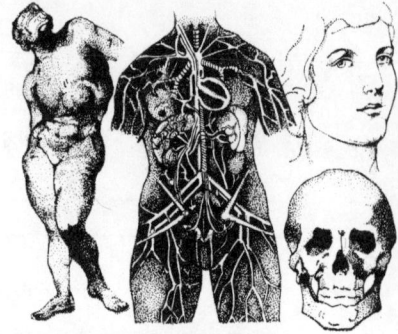

THE SENSE OF TOUCH

The sense of touch, or feeling, is controlled by the skin. Your fingertips are very sensitive parts of your body. Close your eyes for a moment and touch a few objects that you have placed before you, and you will easily understand the powerful sense of touch.

The skin is a very important sense organ. Your skin responds to cold and heat because it has many tiny nerve cells in it. In some parts of the skin, the nerve cells are more sensitive than in other parts. The nerve cells in your skin pick up messages and send them to your brain. Your brain immediately informs you about what you have touched.

Skin has several layers. The outer layer is called the *epidermis*. Any injury to the epidermis can be very painful. If you cut the skin (called a *laceration*) or bang it (called a *bruise*), you may experience bleeding, ruptured blood vessels, and a chance of infection. A blow to your skin which makes it turn black and blue causes the rupture of many blood vessels in that area. The skin also contains small muscles and sweat glands. The *sweat glands* control perspiration, and this is Nature's way of cooling you off when it is hot.

It is important for the skin to be kept clean with the use of soap and water. Not only does soap and water remove dirt and possible germ infection, but it also allows your skin to "breathe" through tiny holes called *pores*. Clogged pores become pimples or blackheads and interfere with the *regulation* of body temperature.

1. What is the function of the skin as a sense organ?

   _____

   _____

2. Why does a bruise turn your skin black and blue?

   _____

   _____

3. What is the function of a *pore?*

   _____

   _____

4. Look up these words in a dictionary and know their meaning:

    regulation   _____
    laceration   _____
    bruise   _____
    sweat gland   _____

5. Describe the parts of your body that may not be overly sensitive to the touch of objects. Explain why:

    _____
    _____

6. What is the *epidermis*?

    _____
    _____

7. What is the difference between a *bruise* and a *laceration*?

    _____
    _____

8. Why is skin cleanliness important?

    _____
    _____

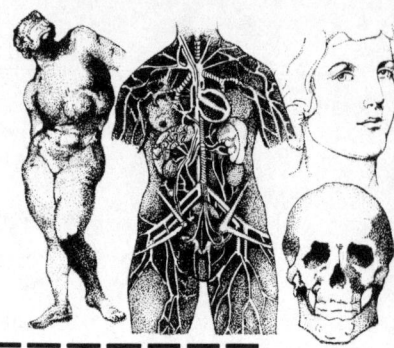

THE SENSE OF SMELL

The sense of smell is a complex process. Not only does it involve your nose, but it also involves your sense of taste. If something has an offensive odor, you won't try to taste it.

The nose is the chief organ used in the sense of smell. Remember, the chief use of the nose is for respiration and the warming of air before it goes to your lungs. However, it is also the smelling agent for your body. Nerve cells in your nose pick up odors and transmit them to the brain for immediate replay to you. When your nose is blocked by a cold, this process is slowed down a bit.

1. What is meant by the word *offensive*? (Look it up in the dictionary.)

   _____

   _____

2. List six offensive odors that you have discovered:

   a. _____   d. _____
   b. _____   e. _____
   c. _____   f. _____

3. How do smell and taste join together to determine odors?

   _____

   _____

4. How does a cold or a blocked nose passage affect your sense of smell?

   _____

   _____

5. List six pleasant odors that you like:

   a. _____   d. _____
   b. _____   e. _____
   c. _____   f. _____

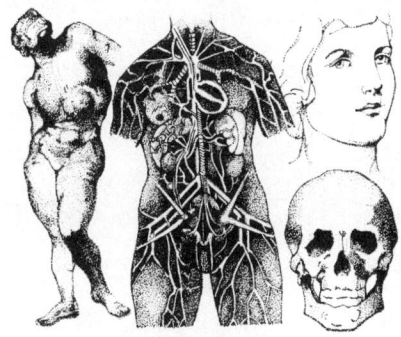

WHICH PART DOES WHAT?

How much do you know about your body? Do you know what certain parts of the body actually do? Try to match each of the functions below with the *correct* body part listed:

1. What part pumps blood?   _____
2. What part digests food?   _____
3. What parts form the skeleton?   _____
4. What part controls your breathing?   _____
5. What part allows you to smell?   _____
6. What part allows you to recognize colors?   _____
7. What part allows you to taste food?   _____
8. What part is tissue that covers your body?   _____
9. What part is the nerve tissue in your head?   _____
10. What part connects your head to your body?   _____
11. What part allows you to grab things?   _____
12. What part allows you to sing?   _____

fingers	stomach	tongue	arteries
mouth	skin	lungs	ribs
nose	ear	toes	vein
heart	neck	bones	tonsils
brain	hip	eye	chest

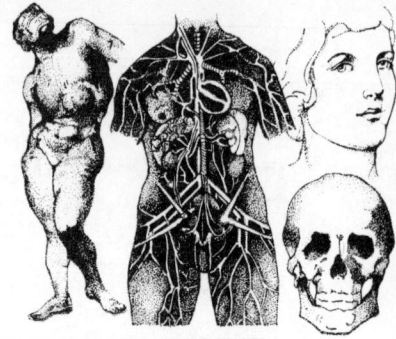

DRUGS AND NARCOTICS

A *drug* is any type of medicine that a doctor may *prescribe* to help cure a person who is ill. A doctor may prescribe a drug to kill germs and stop infection, to make you go to sleep, to relieve pain, and even to make you stay awake. Some drugs are mild and other drugs are very strong. Not all people can take drugs. Some people can only take aspirin because stronger drugs make them sick, dizzy, and weak.

A *narcotic* is also a drug, but a narcotic refers to the more powerful forms of drugs. Powerful types of drugs come from a flower called an *opium poppy*. The drugs from that flower are known as *morphine*, which kills pain, and *heroin*, which can make a person feel and act strangely. In recent years, the term *narcotics* has been used in movies and on television to refer to the illegal use, sale, and transportation of drugs. Most of the narcotics used illegally in this country come from other nations.

If a person uses a drug often, it becomes habit-forming. The person must depend on that drug all the time. The person is then known as a *drug addict*. Because narcotics cost a great deal of money, people who become addicted to them often commit crimes to obtain money to pay for the drugs. Too often, young children become drug users and develop certain physical problems.

A person should only use drugs that will help him in a time of illness or pain. To use drugs constantly as a "kick" or a "thrill" becomes very dangerous and can cripple a person mentally and physically.

1. Define the term *drug*:

   _____

   _____

2. Look up these words in your dictionary and write a definition for each one:

   addict   _____

   morphine   _____

   prescribe   _____

3. What is a *narcotic?*

_____

_____

4. Why does a doctor prescribe drugs?

_____

_____

5. Why are narcotics dangerous to young people?

_____

_____

6. What is an *opium poppy?*

_____

_____

7. How many words can you make from the letters in the word NARCOTIC?

_____

_____

_____

8. What does the drug *morphine* do?

_____

_____

9. What does the drug *heroin* do?

_____

_____

10. Why do some people take drugs as a "kick" or a "thrill"?

_____

_____

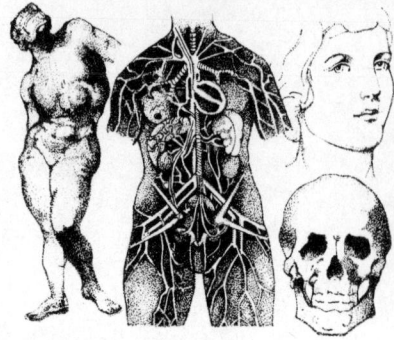

HUMAN BODY MYSTERY PUZZLE

Read each clue and unscramble the letters to form a human body word. Then spell another word from the letters in the circles.

1. give you your height   S N O E B

2. send messages   E V S N E R

3. moistens food   H O T U M

4. harmful   T N A R C C I S O

5. five of them   N E S S E S

6. helps us to shape words   G U N E T O

Circled word is _____.

The Human Body

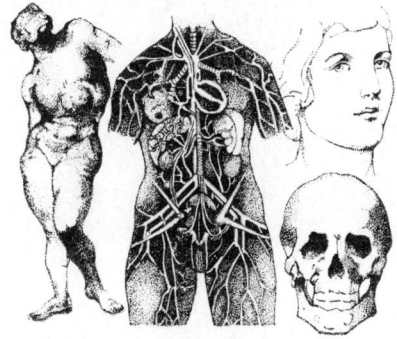

HUMAN BODY ALPHABETIZED WORDS

Write one word that begins with each of the letters listed below. The words must all be related to the human body.

A _____

B _____

C _____

D _____

F _____

G _____

H _____

J _____

L _____

M _____

N _____

O _*oxygen*_____

P _____

R _____

S _____

T _____

V _____

W _____

The Human Body   81

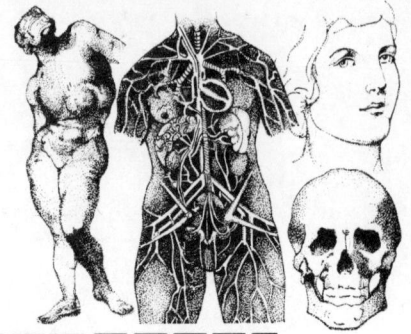

HUMAN BODY WORD FUN

Each of the words listed below the puzzle relates to the human body and good health. See how many of these words you can find. Do you know the definition of each one? If not, use your dictionary to guide you on these special health terms.

```
A H S A L F E C S C L
E Y E I R S T N K H L
P A P A A N O S E E U
R U I E L Z O E L S K
P U S W Q T T N E T S
M I T R A E H O T R H
D Z N N I K S B O A A
S E O T B R A I N E N
G J H C A M O T S H D
A L U N G S B I R E S
```

nose	ear	bones	stomach
disease	brain	lungs	lash
pint	eye	heart	tooth
ribs	toes	skeleton	chest
health	hands	pupil	skin
skull			

The Human Body

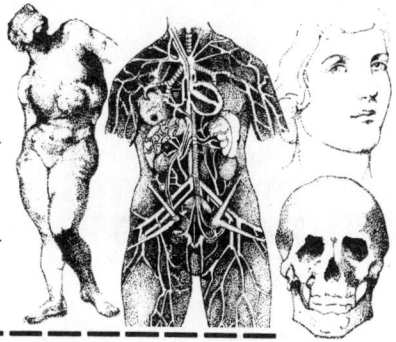

HUMAN BODY SCRAMBLED TERMS

Each of these terms should be familiar to you from this chapter. Look at each set of scrambled letters and rearrange them to spell the correct word.

1. ippul   _____   contracts with light
2. lecls   _____   tiny parts of body
3. siri   _____   color of eye
4. gueont   _____   contains four parts of taste
5. roomt   _____   type of nerve
6. carttcon   _____   to get smaller
7. tacfrreu   _____   to break
8. valisa   _____   moisture
9. cibep   _____   arm muscle
10. rarmow   _____   bone food
11. tuprrue   _____   to break
12. tincefnoi   _____   caused by germ
13. larticgae   _____   pads between bones
14. lapcilyar   _____   blood vessel
15. machots   _____   digests food
16. cumles   _____   moves bones

The Human Body   83

WEATHER

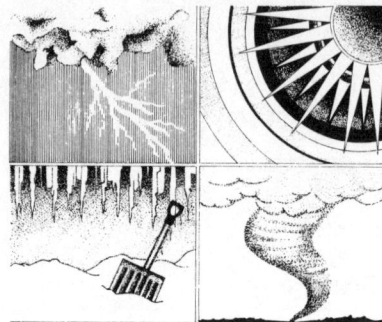

INTRODUCTION TO THE TEACHER

Weather is always an interesting topic of study. Elementary school children are intrigued by Nature's wonders, and weather certainly presents its share of mysteries.

Reading comprehension exercises have been presented in specific related areas which include the atmosphere, clouds, storms (such as hurricanes and tornadoes), forms of weather, and information about the hydrosphere.

Again, basic vocabulary and fact retention are stressed. Each of the drill activities reinforces the material that is presented for retention by the student.

The material here supplements basic information that is found in the elementary science textbook. It helps the child to develop an attitude of inquiry into specific facets of weather information. Each of these activities has been designed to strengthen basic concepts and generalizations on the topic of weather.

Children are always interested in learning about the weather. The exercises in this chapter help to fulfill this objective.

3

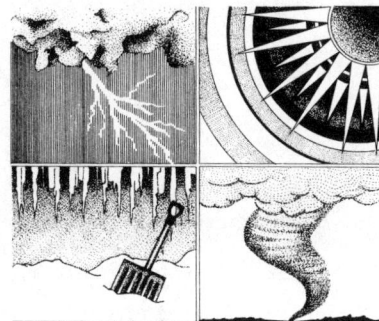

THE ATMOSPHERE

The *atmosphere* is the name given to all of the air surrounding the earth. Scientists, however, have broken down the atmosphere into four separate zones or *spheres* for classification and measurement purposes:

1. *Troposphere*—the first 10 miles above the earth.
   With a temperature of 70 degrees F on earth, it goes to 30 degrees F at 10 miles high. In this area, cumulus clouds form from 1 to 5 miles above the earth's surface. Cirrus clouds are formed about 9 miles high. Planes fly in this space. As you go higher you need oxygen to survive.

2. *Stratosphere*—extends for 50 miles above the troposphere.
   The temperature here goes to –190 degrees F. Some high flying planes (U-2) and some balloons have flown in this sphere.

3. *Ionosphere*—650 miles above the stratosphere.
   The temperature here gets hotter and reaches 2200 degrees F. Many satellites orbit here.

4. *Exosphere*—extends up from the top of the ionosphere.
   The temperature is extremely hot because this is nearer to the sun. The Northern Lights are usually found at this level.

1. List the proper sphere for each of these items by checking the chart above. (Convert feet to miles by dividing total feet by 5000).

   a. jet airplane travel—8 miles high _____
   b. meteors—55 miles _____
   c. radiation belt—250 miles _____
   d. flock of ducks—2 miles _____
   e. altostratus clouds—6000 feet _____
   f. Tiros weather satellite—475 miles _____
   g. U-2 spy plane—90,000 feet _____
   h. Mt. Everest—5100 feet _____

2. Answer these questions from your readings:

a. In which sphere are cirrus clouds found? _____
b. Which sphere is closest to the sun? _____
c. In which sphere is oxygen needed? _____
d. In which sphere are the Northern Lights? _____
e. Which sphere is about 250,000 feet above
   the earth? _____
f. In which sphere do satellites operate? _____
g. In which sphere would the temperature be
   −175 degrees F? _____

3. Using your dictionary, find the definitions of these terms:

a. radiation belt _____
b. cirrus clouds _____
c. artificial satellites _____
d. Northern Lights _____

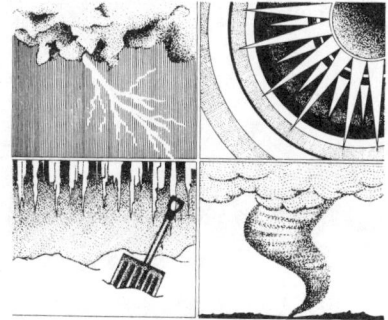

WIND

Wind is moving air. Wind can be described as moving with a force that is calm, light, strong, howling, raging, or very severe. These terms describe the wind's speed and the damage that it can do to soil, trees, land, and property.

Wind direction is measured by a *wind vane*. A wind vane is an arrow device mounted on a pole or on the roof of a building that shifts with the wind blowing on it. Using the points of the compass (North, South, East, and West), you can look at the wind vane to determine what direction the wind is coming from and where it is blowing. A wind sock at an airport is very similar to a wind vane.

Wind speed is measured by an instrument called an *anemometer*. This is also mounted high on a pole or building, and consists of three or four half-spheres that rotate with the wind. The harder the wind blows, the faster the cups rotate and register the speed. The unit of measure for determining wind speed is a *knot*. A knot is equal to about 1.15 miles per hour. A 30-knot wind means it is blowing about $34\frac{1}{2}$ miles per hour. A 40-knot wind means it is blowing at 46 miles per hour. To change knots into miles per hour, you multiply the knot speed by 1.15.

Large winds covering thousands of miles are called a *front*. You may have heard the term "warm front" or "cold front." These fronts affect us in many ways. Winds high in the stratosphere are called *jet streams*. These high winds help airplanes to move faster if they fly with the wind.

Wind is an important source of energy. Wind affects the temperature and the clothes we wear. Wind is something that we are concerned about all the time.

1. Define a *knot*:

   _____

   _____

2. What instrument measures wind direction?

   _____

3. Look up the following terms and write a definition of each one:

    a. warm front   _____

    b. jet stream   _____

    c. wind velocity   _____

4. Change the following knots to miles per hour:

    a. 60 knots   _____

    b. 80 knots   _____

    c. 90 knots   _____

5. How does wind affect what people wear?

_____

_____

6. What instrument measures wind speed?

_____

7. What is a wind sock?

_____

_____

8. How does wind affect crops?

_____

_____

9. What kind of damage do you think a "very severe" windstorm would cause?

_____

_____

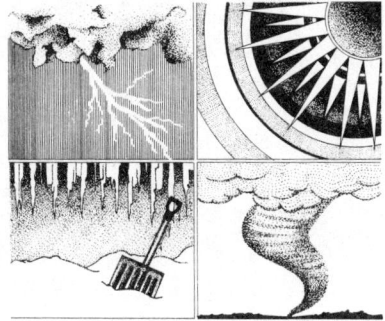

CLOUDS

A *cloud* is a collection of dust particles surrounded by water droplets. Clouds, therefore, consist of water vapor that was once on earth and has *evaporated* into the sky. There are usually some clouds in the sky most of the time, but it is possible to have a bright, sunny day when no clouds are visible.

Cumulus clouds are found closest to the earth and are seen on bright, sunny days. Cumulus clouds can begin at about 500 feet and extend up to 9000 feet. They look like white puffs of cotton in the sky. Cumulus clouds always indicate very good weather.

Stratus clouds appear from about 2000 feet to 6500 feet. These clouds are long, straight, and are in layers, one upon the other. Stratus clouds usually signal stormy weather, rain, or high winds.

Cumulonimbus clouds range from 1000 feet to 40,000 feet high. They look like giant mushrooms in the sky. This type of cloud signifies a thunderstorm. It is even dangerous for an airplane to fly through them.

Altocumulus clouds are way up in the sky, about 25,000 feet and higher. They still look like white puffs of cotton, but they are further out. Altocumulus clouds also indicate very good weather.

Altostratus clouds are high in the sky, about 40,000 feet. They appear as long streaks in the sky and may indicate stormy weather.

The highest cloud formation is called *cirrus* clouds. They appear as long, thin, feathery clouds and can be from 45,000 feet to about 65,000 feet up.

    1. Which cloud would you see:

a. on a clear sunny day close to earth?   _____
b. very high in the sky with rain possibilities?   _____
c. that looks like a mushroom?   _____
d. that is low, long, and straight?   _____

2. Look up these words in your dictionary and write a definition for each one:

   a. evaporation   _____
   b. condensation _____
   c. thunderstorm _____
   d. cirrus clouds _____

3. Why are the stratus clouds alike, even though they are found in different spaces in the sky?

   _____
   _____

4. Which cloud is dangerous to fly through?

   _____

5. Which cloud looks like a small, white puff of cotton?

   _____

6. Which cloud formation looks like a feather?

   _____

7. What is the function of a cloud?

   _____

8. Is it possible to have nice weather without having clouds in the sky?

   _____

9. Look up the word *cloudburst* and see how it relates to our topic of clouds:

   _____
   _____

HURRICANES

A *hurricane* is a very violent windstorm that is common in certain parts of the United States. A hurricane is a large storm that forms over warm water. Hurricanes which reach the United States originate in the area of the Caribbean Sea and move westward in an unpredictable pattern. Some turn northward and move out over the ocean, while others move straight and hit land, like the southern part of the United States.

Hurricanes are very large storms. They are circular in shape like a large donut. The center of the hurricane, which is free of heavy winds, is called the *eye*. This is known as the "calm part" of a hurricane. Some hurricanes have been known to be 600 miles across, and some have lasted for as long as two weeks.

Because hurricanes are very dangerous storms, they can create millions of dollars worth of damage by their path of destruction. They cause very high tides which destroy beach areas and sink ships. Water damage to property can be very high. Winds can reach up to 120 miles per hour, which can level buildings in minutes. Hurricanes can knock out electrical power plants, plunging a city into darkness for days. The wind and rain also *contaminate* the water supply so that people must boil water which they use to drink and cook.

The U.S. Weather Bureau uses special types of airplanes, called Hurricane Hunters, to track the path and determine the severity of a hurricane. Civil Defense teams are alerted to help people *evacuate* an area where a hurricane may strike. Special precautions must be taken if a hurricane alert is sounded. People need to stock up on food, water, and artificial forms of lighting in order to "weather the storm."

1. What are some of the effects of a hurricane?

_____

_____

2. What is meant by the phrase "weather the storm"?

_____

_____

3. What is the center of a hurricane called?

_____

4. Look up these words in your dictionary and write a definition
for each one:

    contaminate   _____

    Civil Defense   _____

    Caribbean Sea   _____

    artificial light   _____

5. How large can some hurricanes be?

_____

6. What is a Hurricane Hunter?

_____

_____

7. How does Civil Defense help people during a hurricane alert?

_____

_____

8. How fast can the winds travel in a hurricane?

_____

9. Where does a hurricane usually start?

_____

10. How is a hurricane shaped?

_____

11. See how many words you can make from letters in the word
H U R R I C A N E:

_____

_____

_____

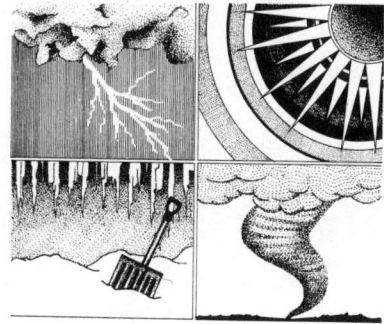

TORNADOES

A *tornado* is another very violent storm that occurs in the United States. Tornadoes are very large windstorms which begin over land. The air swirls and turns around in circles when two air masses meet. The circles swirl faster and get bigger to form a tall, funnel-shaped mass of moving air. Tornadoes are not very wide, but winds in a tornado can move at speeds up to 600 miles per hour. At this speed winds are very dangerous. The air is so strong in a tornado that it can drive a straw through a piece of wood.

As the funnel-shaped cloud moves across land, it dips down to the ground and touches things like homes, cars, barns, and shopping centers. When it does this, it destroys everything in its path. The center of a tornado has less pressure than the outside of the tornado. Whatever the tornado touches collapses like a pile of matchsticks. It can lift houses completely off the ground and move them many yards away. It can toss cars around like toys. In one tornado in Florida recently, mail from a post office which had been damaged was found 150 miles away.

There is very little protection against a tornado except to seek safety in the basement of your home. Some homes do not have basements so people are *evacuated* to a stronger type of building like a school or armory. Rain accompanies a tornado as it sucks water up from rivers and ponds along its path. A tornado sounds like a large freight train passing through. Tornadoes knock down power lines, block highways with wreckage, and uproot many trees.

Civil Defense workers are trained to help people during a tornado alert.

1. How is a tornado different from a hurricane?

   _____

   _____

2. What shape does a tornado take?

   _____

3. What type of damage can a tornado do?

_____

_____

4. Look up these words in your dictionary and write a definition for each one:

evacuate _____

disaster _____

pressure _____

funnel _____

5. How fast can winds in a tornado travel?

_____

6. Where should you seek shelter during a tornado alert?

_____

7. Where does a tornado usually begin?

_____

8. How many words can you make from the letters in the word T O R N A D O?

_____

_____

_____

LIGHTNING AND THUNDER

Lightning is a very dangerous form of electricity. For many years, people thought that lightning was a form of God's punishment. Today we know that lightning is caused by water drops in the air that *collide* with each other. This causes electricity to jump around the sky.

The lightning may jump from one cloud to another, as most often happens, or it may jump to the ground. Lightning often strikes the tallest object on the ground, like a tree or large building. If lightning hits a tree, the tree is killed instantly. When lightning hits a forest, it may start a forest fire. Sometimes people are killed by lightning. There have been occasions when people have sought shelter underneath a tree during a thunderstorm only to be killed by lightning. It is very dangerous to be underneath a tree or in an open boat when lightning occurs. The best place to be is inside a building away from windows.

Thunder is the noise lightning makes as it passes through the sky. Thunder occurs when lightning passes through the air and creates a small *vacuum*. When the air rolls back into the space where the lightning has passed through, it crashes together with a loud sound. Thunder is not harmful, although it does hurt some people who have sensitive eardrums. Thunder can rattle dishes in your home and shake the walls of your house.

Lightning is usually followed by thunder. When you hear the thunder soon after you see the lightning, you know that the storm is very close to you. That is the time to seek safety.

1. Why is thunder not considered a danger?

_____

_____

2. How is lightning formed?

_____

_____

3. How is thunder formed?

_____

_____

4. Look up these words in your dictionary and write a definition for each one:

vacuum   _____

electricity   _____

forest fire   _____

thunderstorm   _____

5. What safety measures should you take if you are in an open area and you see lightning flashing?

_____

_____

6. How do some forest fires start?

_____

_____

7. Alphabetize these words, using numbers 1-9.

_____thunder   _____fire

_____streak   _____flashes

_____lightning   _____cloud

_____vacuum   _____safety

_____electricity

8. See how many words you can make from the letters in the word L I G H T N I N G:

_____

_____

_____

RELATED WEATHER HAPPENINGS

There are many interesting things associated with weather.

A *cyclone* is a dust storm which travels in swirling circles across land. It picks up dust, dirt, and brush, and swirls it around very fast, making it difficult to breathe. Cyclones occur over land in the western part of the United States. They are not as large as tornadoes but they can cause a great deal of damage.

A *typhoon* is a hurricane that forms over water. It sometimes hits land. Typhoons, like hurricanes, are large storms which pack high winds and carry a lot of rain. Japan is a nation that has experienced many typhoons. Typhoons are dangerous for ships at sea.

Unlike the storms described above, a *rainbow* is a more pleasant feature of weather. Light from the sun travels to the earth in fairly straight lines. Light usually appears white, but it is actually composed of seven different colors which are called the *color spectrum*. The colors always appear in this order: red, orange, yellow, green, blue, indigo (a dark, inky blue), and violet. Rain separates the light into colors and we see the different colors rather than just white light. A rainbow is a half-circle, or *hemisphere*, but we only see part of it since we are on the ground.

Sometimes you can see a rainbow when water is sprinkling on a lawn. The rainbow is considered a good luck sign, and people say that there is always a "pot of gold" at the end of a rainbow.

1. Is a cyclone like a tornado? Explain:

_____

_____

2. What is a typhoon?

_____

_____

3. What country has been hit by typhoons many times?

_____

4. Write a definition of the word *spectrum*:

_____

_____

5. List the colors of the rainbow in the order in which they appear:

_____

_____

6. How can you make a rainbow?

_____

_____

7. Why do we only see part of a rainbow?

_____

_____

8. Where are cyclones found in the United States?

_____

_____

9. Why is a rainbow considered a lucky sign?

_____

_____

10. See how many words you can make out of the letters in the word R A I N B O W:

_____

_____

_____

EROSION

One of the constant weather changes that affect the earth is called *erosion.* Basically, erosion is the moving of material from one place to another. This type of movement is caused by wind, rain, snow, and ice, as well as by rivers, floods, tornadoes, and hurricanes. Whenever some force moves dirt, rocks, and trees, erosion is taking place.

However, another type of weather change occurs before erosion takes place. This is called *weathering*, which is the breaking down of rocks and soil into smaller pieces. Weathering is also caused by many forces, including freezing, the growth of roots of plants, and the movements of animals, wind, and water. When rocks break into smaller pieces, the process is called *decomposition*. When something decomposes, it is broken up into smaller particles.

Weathering helps erosion by allowing the forces to move the material more easily. Rivers and flash floods carry away tons of dirt and rock and deposit it elsewhere. Wind blows dust, sand, and topsoil around to other locations. Waterfalls cause erosion. Tides cause erosion. Tornadoes can pick things up and deposit them miles away.

One of the many things that is done to prevent erosion is the planting of trees. Another is building dams and causing water to travel along a prescribed path. Some erosion, however, cannot be stopped at all.

Weathering, decomposition, and erosion are forms of matter changes. Erosion is necessary for the cycle of weather, but in some cases erosion protection is a necessary goal for farmers, geologists, and other scientists.

1. What is weathering?

   _____

   _____

2. What forces can cause weathering?

   _____

   _____

3. What is erosion?

_____

_____

4. What forces cause erosion?

_____

_____

5. How does freezing affect weathering?

_____

_____

6. What is decomposition?

_____

_____

7. How can man protect himself against erosion?

_____

_____

8. How many words can you make from the letters in the word
   W E A T H E R?

_____

_____

9. How do storms create erosion?

_____

_____

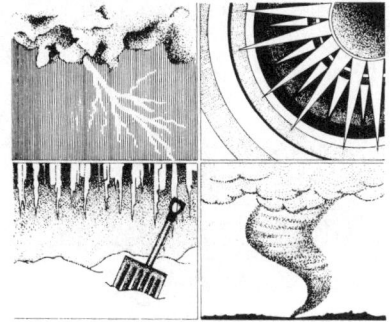

HYDROSPHERE INFORMATION

The *hydrosphere* consists of all the water in the world. It includes oceans, seas, lakes, ponds, streams, rivers, and water vapor. The hydrosphere makes up a large percentage of the surface area of the earth. About 75 percent of the earth is covered by water.

1. Why is the hydrosphere important?

_____

_____

2. What are some very basic uses of water?

a._____   d._____

b._____   e._____

c._____   f._____

3. What is the *water cycle*?

_____

_____

4. List five large oceans:

a._____   d._____

b._____   e._____

c._____

5. What is the name of the river closest to your home?

_____

6. What is the name of the lake or pond closest to your home?

_____

7. Waterways have always been used as boundaries between nations or states. Why do you think this is so?

_____

_____

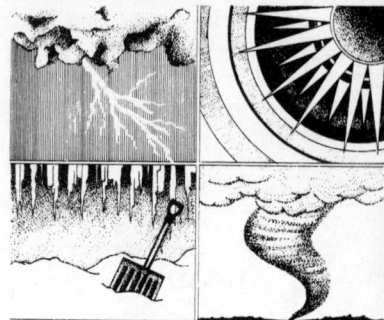

WEATHER MYSTERY PUZZLE

Read each clue and unscramble the letters to form a weather word. Then spell another word from the letters in the circles.

1. units of measure   S K O N T

2. noisy   D U H N T R E

3. does great damage   D O L F O

4. shooting star   R E T M E O

5. damp   M U D I H

6. like soft white flakes   Y O S W N

Circled word is _____.

WEATHER ALPHABETIZED WORDS

Think of a word beginning with each of the letters listed. Be sure your word is related to weather in some way.

A _____

B _____

C _____

D _____

E _____

F _____

G _____

H _____

I _ _ice_ _____

L _____

M _____

N _____

O _____

P _____

R _____

S _____

T _____

V _____

W _____

WEATHER WORD FUN

Can you find these weather terms?

```
A  T  O  N  K  T  N  O  R  F  C  A
S  T  Z  D  A  M  P  J  H  H  O  T
C  U  M  U  L  U  S  S  A  U  O  N
S  D  O  O  L  F  O  P  Q  R  L  A
U  I  W  L  S  R  M  H  R  R  O  E
R  R  F  C  I  P  S  E  K  I  D  C
R  R  E  T  X  C  H  R  Z  C  A  O
I  O  D  T  L  T  V  E  N  A  N  E
C  T  N  E  A  K  A  L  R  N  R  L
P  O  I  E  J  A  M  L  E  E  O  C
H  G  W  L  V  E  L  O  C  I  T  Y
N  O  O  S  N  O  M  A  L  O  O  C
E  R  E  H  P  S  O  P  O  R  T  A
```

cool	damp	wind	torrid
tornado	knot	cloud	flood
cumulus	velocity	weather	cirrus
monsoon	hot	Tiros	hurricane
cycle	sphere	front	sleet
atmosphere	troposphere	ocean	

WEATHER SCRAMBLED TERMS

These scrambled terms all have to do with weather. Read the clue and write down the correct word.

1. ticderino   _____ which way
2. rhsedeyphor   _____ has to do with water
3. tehaerw   _____ changes all the time
4. neryeg   _____ all around us
5. arehricun   _____ violent storm
6. dolof   _____ causes great water damage
7. dwin   _____ unseen force
8. mepertasoh   _____ all around us
9. acone   _____ a large home
10. peraovtonia   _____ forms clouds
11. tonk   _____ speed measurement
12. darotno   _____ causes wind damage
13. roteme   _____ falls from the sky
14. diumh   _____ damp
15. vioyetcl   _____ speed

THE SOLAR SYSTEM

INTRODUCTION TO THE TEACHER

The study of space and our solar system has received renewed emphasis in elementary school science. This chapter contains activities and games that stress basic information about the planets, the moon, and the earth's surface.

Reading comprehension and interpretation exercises build vocabulary development, inference skills, research skills, and logical reasoning. Some mathematical reasoning is also included.

The puzzles also reinforce basic knowledge and aim to strengthen facts, concepts, and generalizations related to this important unit of study.

Again, following the pages in the numerical order presented gives a broader base for the student's understanding. However, it is possible to start at any page of the chapter.

Included in this section are anagrams, word order discovery exercises, and alphabetization review exercises. Most students find the study of the earth and the solar system a fascinating area. The activities in this section help to promote interest in this topic and challenge students to do further research and study of solar system facts.

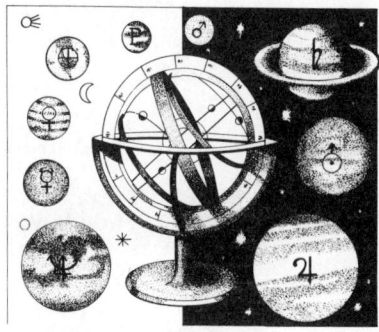

THE PLANETS

The *solar system* consists of the sun and nine known planets. The first four planets are known as the *inner planets* because they are closest to the sun. Their names (in order from the sun) are Mercury, Venus, Earth, and Mars.

The remaining five planets are called the *distant planets*. They are Jupiter, Saturn, Uranus, Neptune, and Pluto. Each planet *rotates* (spins around) on its *axis*, which is an imaginary line through the planet. As it rotates the planet also revolves around the sun on a path called an *orbit*.

Mercury is the smallest planet. It revolves around the sun in 88 days. *Venus* is the second planet and it takes 243 days to revolve around the sun. *Earth* is the third planet and its revolution around the sun takes 365 days. *Mars*, sometimes called "the red planet," has a revolution period of 687 days. *Jupiter* is the largest planet and it takes 11.9 years to go around the sun. *Saturn*, the planet with the rings, is the sixth planet. It takes 29.5 years to go around the sun. *Uranus* is a gaseous planet and it takes 84 years to orbit the sun. *Neptune*, the eighth planet, takes 165 years to orbit the sun. *Pluto*, the ninth planet, takes 248 years to orbit the sun. Pluto is so far away that very little is really known about it.

The solar system also contains *comets*, bodies of dust and ice with long, swirling tails. *Meteoroids*, fragments of a comet, are also found in space and can be photographed. Meteoroids that reach the earth's atmosphere are called *meteors*. When a meteor hits the earth it is called a *meteorite*. Most meteors contain iron. Scientists enjoy studying meteors because they give them much information about outer space.

1. List the nine planets in the solar system in order from the sun:

_____

_____

_____

2. What is the difference between a meteor and a meteoroid?

_____

_____

3. A meteor that hits the earth is called a _____ .

4. How long does it take for the following planets to orbit the sun?

   Mercury   _____   Uranus   _____
   Pluto   _____   Earth   _____
   Mars   _____   Jupiter   _____

5. Make as many words as you can out of the letters in the word M E T E O R:

   _____

   _____

   _____

6. List the inner planets:

   _____

   _____

7. What is an *axis*?

   _____

   _____

8. What is an *orbit*?

   _____

   _____

9. Define *rotate*:

   _____

   _____

10. List the distant gaseous planets:

   _____

   _____

OUR PLANET—EARTH

The planet we live on is called Earth. It is the third planet from the sun and it is almost spherical in shape. The Earth is about 8000 miles in diameter. It is about 25,000 miles around its outer surface. The Earth is about twice as large as Mars and just a little larger than Venus, its other neighboring planet. The Earth is approximately 93 million miles away from the sun.

As far as we now know, Earth is the only planet containing life. This is because it is just the right distance from the sun. The sun does not scorch the land and there is a blanket of air around the Earth to provide oxygen for its inhabitants.

The Earth is tilted on its axis at an angle of 23.5 degrees. The Earth *rotates* on its axis once every 24 hours. This is called an *earth day*. While the Earth turns on its axis every day, it also follows an orbit around the sun. This orbit is called a *revolution* and it takes 365¼ earth days to complete. This is called a *solar year*. A *rotation* means once around Earth's axis (24 hours), and a *revolution* means once around the sun (365¼ days).

Day and night on Earth are governed by the position of the Earth as it faces the sun. In the northern hemisphere of the Earth there are approximately 12 hours of daylight and 12 hours of darkness from March to September. There are less than 12 hours of daylight between September and March.

To measure time, imaginary lines are drawn on the Earth. These lines are called *longitude* and *latitude*. Longitude divides the earth into units from east to west, which are sometimes called *meridians*. Latitude lines are used to measure north and south from the equator. The equator is 0 degrees and latitude lines are 15 degrees apart north and south of the equator. This measurement helps navigators in ships and in planes to plot their courses.

1. The Earth is _____ miles from the sun.

2. *Rotation* means:

_____

_____

3. *Revolution* means:

_____

_____

4. The Earth is about _____ miles through the center.

5. A solar year is _____ days long.

6. An earth day is _____ hours long.

7. The Earth is tilted at an angle of _____ degrees.

8. How many miles around is the Earth? _____.

9. How are day and night governed on Earth?

_____

_____

10. Lines dividing the Earth to the north and south from the equator are called _____.

11. Lines dividing the earth from east to west are called _____ or _____.

12. What are these lines used for?

_____

_____

13. The months when there are approximately 12 hours of daylight and 12 hours of darkness in the northern hemisphere are between _____ and _____.

DISCOVER THIS PLANET

Look at each set of scrambled letters. Then read the clue. Write the correct word in the spaces provided. When you have finished, take all of the letters in the circles and write them on the line below to spell the name of one of the planets.

1. T S A R T   ◯ _ ◯ _ _ _   (to begin)

2. S U C M T O   _ _ _ ◯ _ _   (something that happens the same over the years)

3. L B U P M R E   _ _ ◯ _ _ _ ◯   (fixes faucets)

4. I N S R A I   _ _ _ _ _ ◯   (a dried grape)

The planet is _____.

Can you draw a picture of this planet?

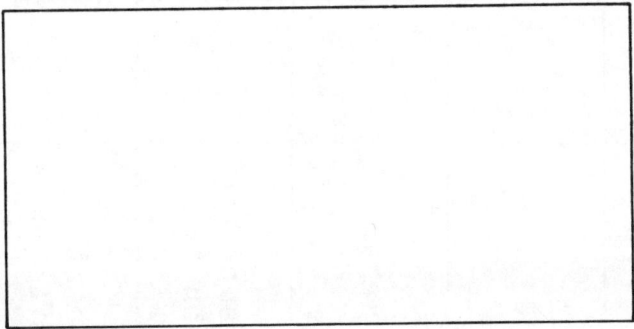

PHYSICAL PROPERTIES OF THE PLANETS

	Mercury	Venus	Earth	Mars	Jupiter	Saturn	Uranus	Neptune	Pluto
Distance from the Sun									
Diameter									
Temperature									
Number of Days for Orbit									
Number of Known Satellites									
Important Features									

(Find the necessary information in your science book or in an encyclopedia.)

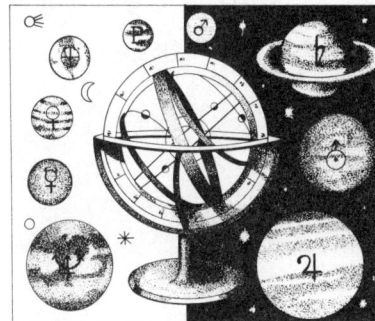

LEARNING ABOUT THE MOON

The *moon* is the natural *satellite* of the Earth. It is located about 240,000 miles from Earth. The moon rotates around the Earth every 29½ days. This period of time is from one new moon to the next new moon. This period is also called a *month*.

When the Earth and the moon come into a direct line with the sun, an *eclipse* occurs and a shadow is cast on the moon by the Earth, or on the Earth by the moon. There are two kinds of eclipses—a *lunar eclipse* and a *solar eclipse*. An eclipse of the moon is called a lunar eclipse. This occurs when the sun, Earth, and moon are lined up so that the moon is in the Earth's shadow. A *solar eclipse* occurs when the moon is directly between the Earth and the sun. During a solar eclipse, the moon shuts out the sun's rays over part of the Earth. Only a small part of the Earth experiences a total solar eclipse because the moon is so much smaller than the Earth.

We see the moon in four different shapes called *phases*. The first phase that we see of the moon is part of the left-hand side, which is called the *first quarter*. The second phase is the total moon, or *full moon*. Next we see part of the right-hand side of the moon, which is called the *last quarter*. The last phase is the *crescent moon*, which looks like a small arc of a circle.

There is no air on the moon and our recent moon landings have discovered no life there. The moon does, however, control the tides on the Earth by its force of gravity. The moon's gravity is one-sixth of the Earth's gravity. Therefore, if you were on the moon, you would divide your present weight by 6. Some overweight people would like that!

1. What is the *moon*?

   _____

   _____

2. List the *phases* of the moon:

   a. _____   c. _____
   b. _____   d. _____

3. What is an *eclipse*?

_____

_____

4. Describe a *solar eclipse*:

_____

_____

5. How long is the orbit of the moon around the earth?

_____

6. How far away is the moon from the earth?

_____

7. Describe a lunar eclipse:

_____

_____

8. What phase is the full moon?

_____

9. Find your weight on the moon. Divide your weight by 6 and write your answer here: _____ pounds.

10. How do we know for certain that there is no air or life on the moon?

_____

_____

11. The word for moon in Latin is *luna*. Words like *lunatic* and *lunacy* come from this root word. Look up these words and find out what they mean:

_____

_____

THE MOON LANDING

Neil Armstrong was the first American astronaut to step on the moon in July 1969. The space program had fulfilled an important objective that was established by President John F. Kennedy. This objective was to land a man on the moon before the end of the 1960s.

This spectacular feat combined the talents of hundreds of people, including scientists, engineers, doctors, designers, radar technicians, teachers, and many other people in the military and civilian forces. The three astronauts who first traveled to the moon returned safely to earth by a parachute landing in the Pacific Ocean. America honored the three heroes with many parades, banquets, and decorations.

1. In what month and year did the American astronauts first land on the moon?

   _____

2. Where did the astronauts land upon their return to earth?

   _____

3. What was the name of the first American on the moon?

   _____

4. How many astronauts were involved on this trip?

   _____

5. List some of the people who were responsible for this successful trip:

   _____

   _____

6. What American President backed this important space achievement?

   _____

ROCKET IN ORBIT

Put the rocket successfully into orbit. If you meet a barrier on the way, you must start over again. Can you do this on the first try?

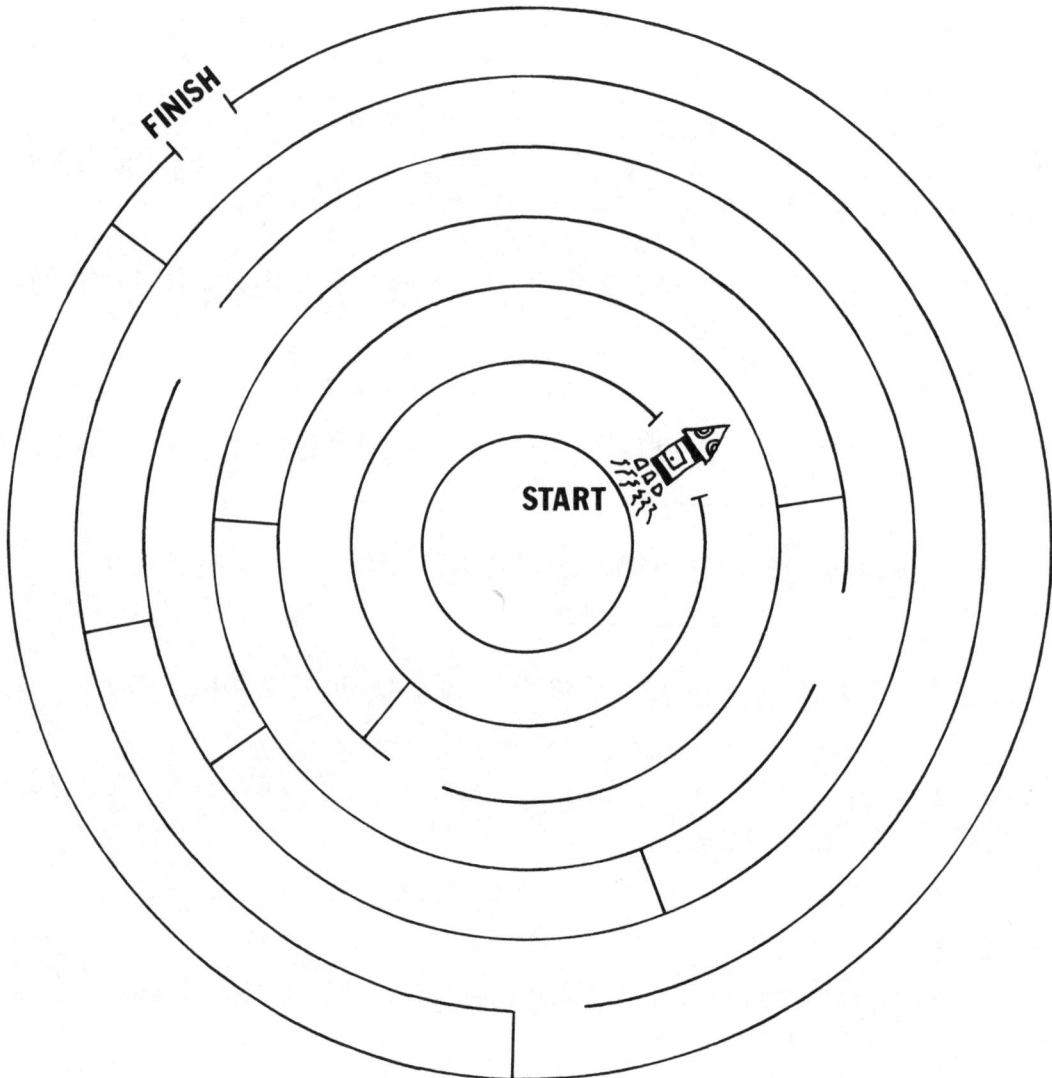

FINISH

START

The Solar System

STUDYING THE EARTH'S SURFACE

The study of the development and structure of the earth's crust, rocks, and fossils is called *geology*. A person who does this type of study is called a *geologist*. A geologist is concerned with all types of matter, but he or she is mainly interested in rocks and their formation and uses.

The geological study of the earth is sometimes called *earth science*. However, earth science is a much broader term, covering many more areas of study than what is included in geology. Geologists learn a great deal about the earth by *observation*. Geologists observe formations of rock and their characteristics. They are concerned with the minerals that are found in different parts of the earth's surface. As they study, they make *theories* (logical conclusions) about what they have learned. They observe, test, experiment, and apply their theories to understand the earth in a scientific way.

Studying the earth's rocks and minerals is done so that man can live better and use the resources in the earth. Because scientists have been studying the earth for thousands of years, their efforts have allowed us to use matter in a positive way. We use certain kinds of stone and rock to construct buildings that will last a long time. We use minerals to make products that we use in everyday life. We apply some of the scientists' theories to make us healthier and more able to adapt to our environment.

The efforts of the scientist help us to understand the earth and learn how we can use natural resources to make our lives pleasant and enjoyable.

1. The study of rocks and minerals is called _____.

2. Scientists make *theories* from their *observations*. Explain this statement:

   _____

   _____

3. Define the word *adapt*:

_____

_____

4. What is a *theory*?

_____

_____

5. Why is the study of geology important?

_____

_____

6. What does a geologist do?

_____

_____

7. See how many words you can make from the letters in the word G E O L O G Y:

_____

_____

_____

8. What is a *fossil*?

_____

_____

9. What is the difference between geology and earth science?

_____

_____

10. Why do geologists observe, test, and experiment?

_____

_____

REVIEWING THE SPHERES

You have learned several terms with the word *sphere* in them. Let us review these terms. Read each statement below and then select the proper "sphere word" that fits the definition. Write the word in the blank line next to the definition it fits.

1. name given to water portion of the earth _____

2. the area on earth where all living things exist _____

3. name for the outer crust of the earth _____

4. air in the first 10 miles above the earth _____

5. a name for all of the air that surrounds the earth _____

6. name for half of a sphere _____

7. air that begins at 60 miles above the earth's surface _____

8. air from the top of the ionosphere up _____

9. air that is above the stratosphere _____

troposphere	hydrosphere	atmosphere
hemisphere	ionosphere	exosphere
biosphere	lithosphere	stratosphere

UNDERSTANDING SOLAR SYSTEM TERMS

Read each statement below. Then find the correct answer in the column of words at the right. Unscramble the letters to respell the word correctly and write it in front of the statement. (The scrambled words are not in any particular order and you may use the same answer twice.)

_____ 1. natural satellite of earth

_____ 2. smallest planet in our solar system

_____ 3. a large burning star

_____ 4. planet with a ring around it

_____ 5. first planet in the solar system

_____ 6. largest planet in the solar system

_____ 7. whirling ball of fire with a tail

_____ 8. planet that has animal and human life

_____ 9. large rock that hurtles toward earth

_____10. planet next to ours that may have life

_____11. partial blocking of sun or moon

_____12. known as the "red planet"

_____13. distant suns

_____14. a grouping of solar systems

s r a t s

r a m s

m o n o

s p i e l e c

r e e t o m

u n s

t u l o p

s e v u n

r e m y u r c

n a t u r s

m e t o c

t i p u j e r

r a t e h

l a g x a y

NAME _____

GRADE _____

DATE _____

TEACHER _____

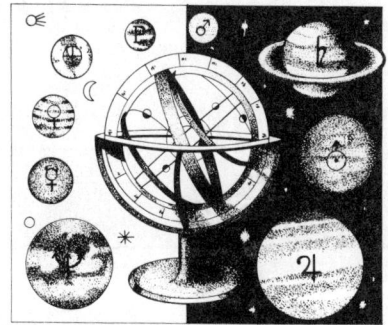

LOOKING FOR WORDS

Look at the words below. Try to see how many words you can make from the letters in each. You can combine the letters in any way as long as they spell a word correctly.

A S T R O N O M E R

(Examples: *at, art, are)* _____

_____

_____

_____

(Make at least 20 words.)

E N V I R O N M E N T

_____

_____

_____

_____

(Make at least 40 words.)

P L A N E T S

_____

_____

_____

_____

(Make at least 16 words.)

SOLAR SYSTEM MYSTERY PUZZLE

Unscramble the letters to form a word. Form another word that relates to the solar system from the letters in the circles.

1. distant sun   R   A   T   S

2. nine of them   S   T   A   N   L   E   P

3. has a tail on it   M   E   C   T   O

4. a path   T   R   I   B   O

5. next to earth   O   M   O   N

6. to spin around once N   A   T   I   O   T   O   R

7. goes up in space   T   R   O   E   K   C

8. fourth planet   R   A   M   S

9. a type of weather   Y   U   N   S   N

Circled word is _____.

SOLAR SYSTEM SCRAMBLED TERMS

These scrambled words on the solar system should be familiar to you. Unscramble the letters and write the word in the blank space provided.

1. teplsan	_____	nine of them
2. loveriutno	_____	once around something
3. vinueers	_____	we are exploring it
4. heart	_____	where we live
5. torib	_____	a path
6. tarooint	_____	turning around
7. lesetpoce	_____	sees things far away
8. reay	_____	period of time
9. naystorom	_____	study of solar system
10. rams	_____	fourth planet
11. nevus	_____	second planet
12. capes	_____	beyond the earth
13. mastroerno	_____	a scientist
14. onom	_____	natural satellite
15. nus	_____	closest star
16. layagx	_____	large area of space
17. tasrnotau	_____	space explorer

MEASUREMENT AND TIME

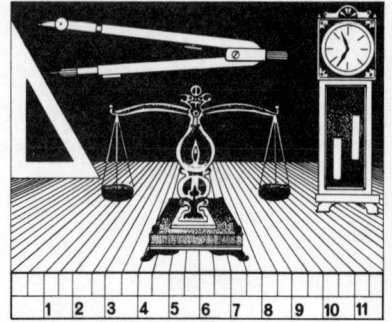

5

INTRODUCTION TO THE TEACHER

This chapter is unique in that it contains many exercises on the topic of measurement and time, which are not developed in great detail in the general elementary science textbook. This section gives the students practice in planning menus, understanding temperature, comparing ocean and land areas, checking temperatures through graph interpretation, and learning about measuring instruments.

The reading comprehension exercises develop basic referential and analogical thinking. The metric system is fully discussed and practical applications of decimal and metric system comparisons are also presented. Decoding skills, anagrams, and vocabulary terms are stressed.

It is important for children to fully comprehend and master the activities in this chapter in order to gain a proper understanding of measurement and time. The skills they will develop will help them to prepare for the "metric" world.

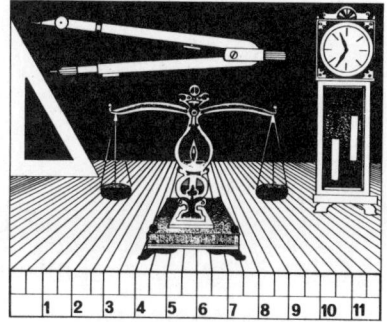

THE MEASUREMENT OF TIME

Time is a strange science term. Time cannot be seen or heard and it cannot be weighed. It cannot be touched. Time is not matter. Time can go ahead but it cannot go back. Time is indeed a strange science concept.

Time is based on the *earth day*, which is 24 hours long, the time it takes for the earth to rotate once around its axis. People had to divide the 24 hours, or one day, into shorter periods for accurate measurement. The first 12 hours are called A.M., and they begin at 12:01, just after midnight. From 12:01 after noontime, the next 12 hours are called P.M. The day is still a long *interval* of time, so scientists broke it down further into hours. Each hour is divided into 60 minutes and each minute is divided into 60 seconds. Now we can have a very accurate measurement of time.

Today, time can be broken down even further because we have electronic means of measurement. *Milliseconds* and *microseconds* are very short intervals of time.

Longitude and *latitude* help with the measurement of time. The distance between longitudes is 15 degrees and this represents one hour of time. So, for every 15 degrees as we travel either east or west on the globe, there is a difference of one hour. The 0 longitude line goes through Greenwich, England, and as we move westward an additional hour of time is added for every 15 degrees.

1. Write a definition for the word *time*:

_____

_____

2. How do longitude and latitude help in determining time?

_____

_____

3. Time is based on the _____.

4. List the hours for the P.M. time interval:

_____

5. List the hours for the A.M. time interval:

_____

6. Look up these words in your dictionary and write a definition for each one:

    a. interval   _____
    b. microsecond   _____
    c. latitude   _____

7. Explain what happens in time as you move every 15 degrees westward from the 0 meridian in England:

_____

_____

8. What are some things that are very dependent on an accurate measurement of time?

    Example: basketball games

    a. _____
    b. _____
    c. _____
    d. _____

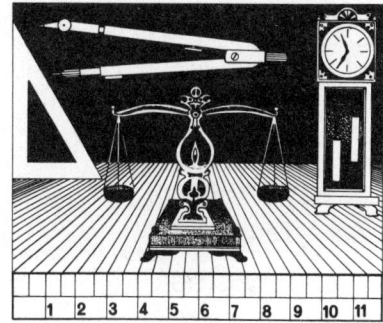

NAME _____   DATE _____

GRADE _____   TEACHER _____

TEMPERATURE

Temperature is the measure of heat or cold in any substance and it is measured by a *thermometer*. For many years we have been using a Fahrenheit thermometer where freezing is 32 degrees and boiling is 212 degrees. However, with the switch to a Celsius (or Centigrade) type of thermometer, freezing is 0 degrees and boiling is 100 degrees.

There is an easy way to convert Fahrenheit into Celsius temperature. Basically, you subtract 30 from the Fahrenheit temperature and divide the remainder by 2.

Example: 70° F minus 30 equals 40 ... divided by 2 equals 20° C. Therefore, 70° Fahrenheit is equal to 20° Celsius.

Using this formula, change these Fahrenheit temperatures to Celsius:

1. 200° F equals _____ C
2. 150° F equals _____ C
3. 40° F equals _____ C
4. 100° F equals _____ C
5. 50° F equals _____ C
6. 90° F equals _____ C
7. 72° F equals _____ C
8. 60° F equals _____ C
9. 30° F equals _____ C
10. 210° F equals _____ C

Measurement and Time   **129**

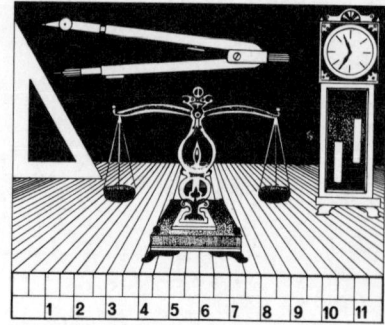

CALORIE COUNT

All food contains *calories*, which are a measurement of the energy in food. Look at the breakfast serving below for both Bob and John. Then look at the listing of foods with their average calorie equivalents. Which boy has more calories in his breakfast?

Bob
2 slices of white bread
½ of an orange
1 cup of corn flakes
1 glass of milk
1 pat of butter

John
I slice of bread
1 pat of butter
½ cup of corn flakes
1 glass of milk
1 egg

Food	*Calories*
corn flakes (cup)	80
white bread (slice)	75
butter (1 pat)	100
egg (one)	70
milk (glass)	170
orange	80

Answer _____

Make up a luncheon menu, not to exceed 500 calories, using the foods listed below as well as the ones above:

1 apple—100   _____
hamburger—100   _____
2 slices of chicken—120   _____
1 cup of baked beans—115   _____
lettuce—5   _____
1 tomato—35   _____
jello (1 cup)—75   _____

Edgar eats all of the fruits and vegetables on the menu for his lunch. How many calories does he consume? _____

Jackie has 1 hamburger, 1 slice of chicken, a cup of jello, and a glass of milk. How many calories are in this lunch? _____

Steve has the same lunch as Edgar but also eats a cup of baked beans. What is his calorie count? _____

Rocky is a heavy eater. For his breakfast he has the following:

      2 slices of bread
      1 glass of milk
      2 pats of butter
      2 eggs
      1 orange

How many calories does Rocky have in his breakfast? _____.

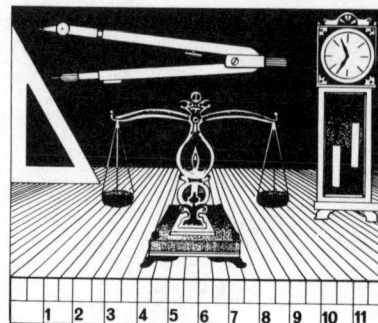

THE METRIC SYSTEM

The *metric system* of measurement has been used in all countries of the world except where English is spoken. Now the metric system has also been adopted by English-speaking nations.

The three common units of measurement in the metric system are the *meter*, the *gram*, and the *liter*. The meter is the unit of measure for *length*. The gram is used for measurements of *weight*. The liter is used to measure *volume*.

We can add prefixes to these words and change them into another type of measurement, either larger or smaller. If we add the prefix *centi* to meter, it becomes *centimeter* or 1/100 of a meter. We can also add *kilo* to meter, and it becomes *kilometer*. *Kilo* means 1000, so a kilometer is 1000 meters. We can add *milli* to gram and we get *milligram*. A milligram is 1/1000 of a gram, which is very small. (Remember, one cent is 1/100 of a dollar. A century is 100 years. You have seen and heard some of these prefixes before.)

A meter is 39.37 inches long. It is 3½ inches longer than a yard. A kilometer, or 1000 meters, is only 0.6 of a mile. A liter is a little over a quart, equal to 1.06 quarts.

Some soft drinks are now being sold by liters. Some states are installing road signs in kilometers to measure distances between cities.

1. List the three common units of measurement in the metric system:

    a. _____
    b. _____
    c. _____

2. A meter is 39.37 inches. How many inches are in 6 meters?

    _____

3. A kilometer is 0.6 of a mile. How many miles are in 12 kilometers? _____

4. Which is larger:

    a. 4 quarts or 3 liters?   _____

    b. 2 meters or 2 yards?   _____

    c. 80 cents or ¾ of a dollar?   _____

5. Write the word for 1000 grams: _____

6. What does a gram measure? _____

7. What does a liter measure? _____

8. What does a meter measure? _____

9. What is now being sold by liters in our stores?

_____

10. Make as many words as you can out of the letters in the word K I L O M E T E R:

_____

_____

_____

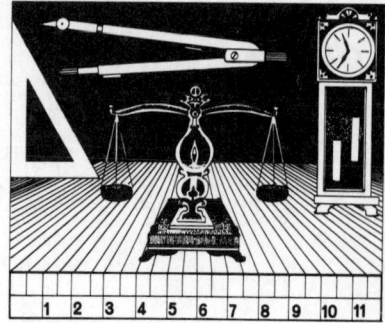

MEASUREMENT CONVERSION

Here are some activities for you to practice measurement conversion. Look at the table and then answer the questions below.

Table of Equivalents

1 mile	= 0.6 kilometer
2.2 pounds	= 1 kilogram
1000 grams	= 1 kilogram
1 inch	= 2.54 centimeters
39.37 inches	= 1 meter

1. Change 10 inches into centimeters. _____
2. Change 4 meters into inches. _____
3. Change 5 kilograms into pounds. _____
4. Change 250 meters into kilometers. _____
5. Change eight miles into kilometers. _____
6. How many miles are in 8.0 kilometers? _____
7. How many inches are in 25.40 centimeters? _____
8. How many grams equal ¼ of a kilogram? _____
9. How many inches are in 6½ meters? _____
10. How many kilograms are in 44 pounds? _____
11. How many centimeters are in 1 foot? _____

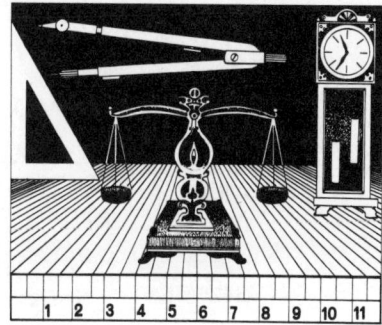

MEASUREMENT AND TIME ANAGRAMS

See how many words you can make from the letters of each of the terms presented below.

1. *measurement* (examples: sure, as, ten) Make at least 25 words.

_____
_____
_____
_____
_____

2. *temperature* (examples: pet, rat) Make at least 20 words.

_____
_____
_____
_____
_____

3. *instruments* (examples: strum, met) Make at least 15 words.

_____
_____
_____
_____
_____

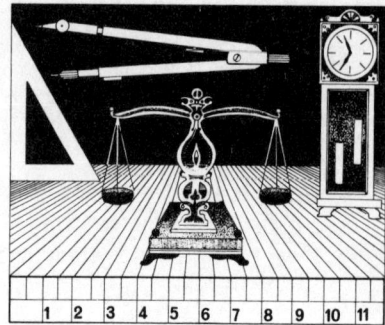

COMPARING AREAS
OF OCEANS AND CONTINENTS

Look at the approximate areas of the oceans and continents listed here. Study them carefully so that you will, be ready to use them in answering the questions listed below.

Ocean Areas

Pacific Ocean .... 64 million square miles
Atlantic Ocean .... 32 million square miles
Indian Ocean .... 28½ million square miles
Arctic Ocean .... 5½ million square miles

Continent Areas

Africa .... 11½ million square miles
Asia .... 17 million square miles
North America .... 9½ million square miles
South America .... 7 million square miles
Europe .... 4 million square miles
Australia .... 3¼ million square miles

Answer these questions by comparing the ocean and continent areas listed above.

1. Which ocean is about four times larger than South America?

_____

2. Which ocean is about six times larger than Africa?

_____

3. What two continents put together are as big as the Indian Ocean?

_____

4. How many square miles do all the oceans total?

_____

5. What continent is about half as big as Asia?

_____

6. How many square miles do all of the continents equal?

_____

7. How many times larger are the combined areas of the oceans in comparison to the combined areas of the continents?

_____

8. What ocean is just slightly larger than the continent of Europe?

_____

9. What ocean is about nine times larger than the continent of Australia?

_____

10. In what continent do you live? _____

11. What ocean is near you? _____

12. Which continent is also an island? _____

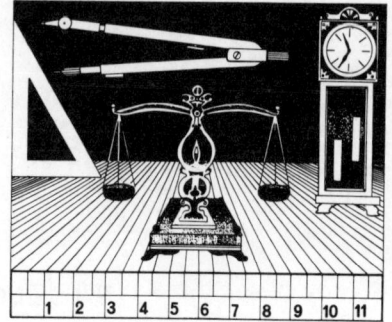

CHECKING TEMPERATURES

Study the temperature chart carefully. Then answer each of the questions listed below.

Time	A.M.							P.M.					
	6	7	8	9	10	11	12	1	2	3	4	5	6
Boston	68°	70°	72°	76°	78°	80°	82°	84°	86°	86°	84°	80°	76°
Miami	80°	82°	84°	86°	88°	90°	92°	96°	98°	99°	99°	96°	90°

1. At what time of day is there the *widest* range of temperature between the two cities? _____

2. Between what times of day is the difference of temperature the *least*? _____

3. At what hours are the temperatures the same in Miami? _____

4. At what hours are the temperatures the same in Boston? _____

5. Between which two hours does the temperature rise the fastest in Boston? _____ In Miami? _____

6. What is the difference in temperature between the two cities at 6 A.M.? _____ 6 P.M.? _____ 12 noon? _____

7. What is the number of degrees that is the *widest* between the two cities? _____

8. What is the number of degrees that is the *least* between the two cities? _____

Measurement and Time

9. At what hour was it the hottest temperature in Miami? _____ In Boston? _____

10. At what hour was it the coolest in Boston? _____ In Miami? _____

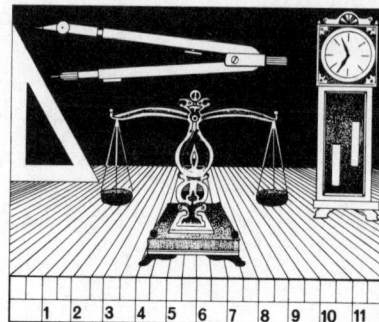

MEASURING INSTRUMENTS

There are hundreds of instruments used in science to measure things accurately. Here are just a few of them. Look at the instrument under Column A and find what you think it measures in Column B. If you have trouble, use your dictionary.

Column A

_____ 1. thermometer
_____ 2. rain gauge
_____ 3. anemometer
_____ 4. barometer
_____ 5. seismograph
_____ 6. spectroscope
_____ 7. hygrometer
_____ 8. odometer
_____ 9. wind vane
_____10. pedometer
_____11. hydrometer
_____12. meter

Column B

a. used to measure the amount of moisture in the air

b. used to measure the direction and intensity of an earthquake

c. used to measure the distance traveled by a vehicle

d. used to measure temperature

e. used to measure the speed of the wind

f. used to measure the number of steps taken by a person

g. used to determine the direction of the wind

h. used to measure air pressure

i. used to measure the amount of rainfall

j. used to measure the density of a fluid (like a battery)

k. used to measure amount of water, gas, or electricity that is used

l. used to measure and record colors of a spectrum

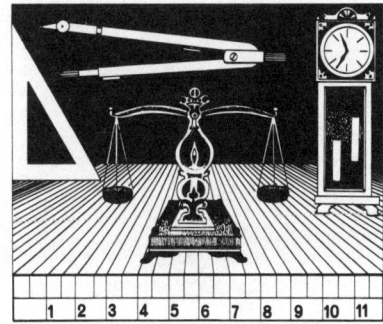

MEASURING TERM ABBREVIATIONS

The terms in the right-hand column are abbreviations for the measuring terms in the first column. Write the correct abbreviation for each of the measuring terms.

1.	_____	Fahrenheit	doz.
2.	_____	teaspoon	hr.
3.	_____	centi	k
4.	_____	cup	qt.
5.	_____	dozen	oz.
6.	_____	tablespoon	pt.
7.	_____	quart	F
8.	_____	Celsius	tsp.
9.	_____	gram	g
10.	_____	hour	C
11.	_____	ounce	c
12.	_____	pound	lb.
13.	_____	pint	min.
14.	_____	minute	m
15.	_____	milli	tbl.
16.	_____	kilo	cp

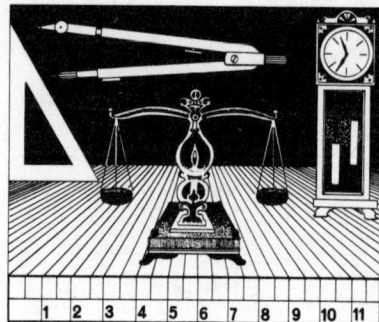

MEASUREMENT AND TIME MYSTERY PUZZLE

Read the clues and unscramble the letters. Put all of the letters in the circles together to form another word.

1. to record   S E A U M R E

2. type of measurement   G R E E D E

3. amount of minutes   E M T I

4. space   E A A R

5. food amount   R O A C L E I

Circled word is _____.

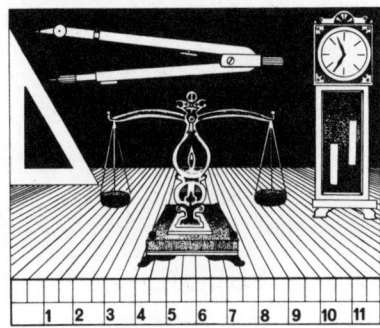

MEASUREMENT AND TIME ALPHABETIZED WORDS

Write a word related to measurement and time that begins with each of the letters listed. Think carefully and see if you can find a word for each letter.

A _____

B _____

C _____

D _degree_____

F _____

H _____

K _____

L _____

M _____

N _____

P _____

R _____

S _____

T _____

W _____

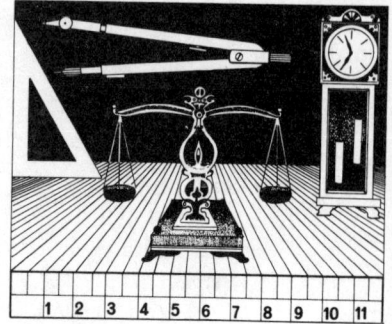

MEASUREMENT AND TIME WORD FUN

Can you find each of the words below in this list of letters?

```
M  C  D  E  D  A  R  G  I  T  N  E  C
I  I  O  A  R  E  A  S  U  N  I  M  R
L  T  L  E  T  I  S  S  A  P  A  C  E
L  C  M  E  U  R  O  P  E  Z  X  K  T
I  R  M  R  S  O  V  E  N  A  T  A  E
O  A  L  G  A  L  B  E  A  K  L  I  M
N  I  O  E  I  A  S  D  V  W  I  N  O
U  N  B  D  S  C  O  L  O  R  S  A  D
E  R  U  T  A  R  E  P  M  E  T  A  E
T  I  E  H  N  E  R  H  A  F  W  H  P
```

minus	eat	Asia	pace
milk	meter	calorie	Centigrade
miles	temperature	Europe	degree
area	Fahrenheit	speed	vane
colors	pedometer	rain	million
Arctic			

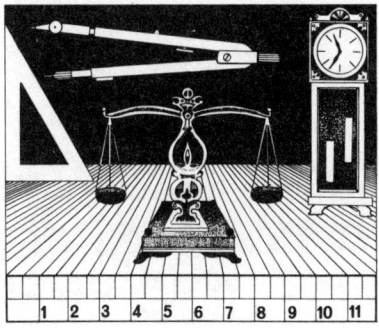

MEASUREMENT SCRAMBLED TERMS

Unscramble these measurement terms. The clue given may help you to determine the word.

#	Scrambled		Clue
1.	rsemaue	_____	to determine specifically
2.	tmparerueet	_____	it affects us daily
3.	coiearl	_____	measurement in food
4.	ccatri	_____	North Pole region
5.	rboareetm	_____	measures air pressure
6.	tinconent	_____	large land region
7.	dopemeter	_____	measures walking distance
8.	Astlruaia	_____	largest island continent
9.	ressprue	_____	force pressing against us
10.	Fiheratenh	_____	type of measuremenh
11.	Erepuo	_____	large land area
12.	arae	_____	large place
13.	temer	_____	longer than a yard
14.	nadsli	_____	surrounded by water
15.	lecissu	_____	type of measurement

CONSERVATION AND ENERGY

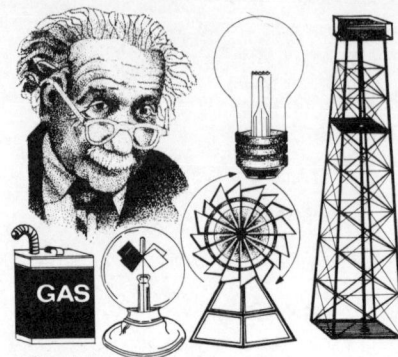

6

INTRODUCTION TO THE TEACHER

Energy and conservation are indeed important areas of concern in this decade. Activities in this chapter stress a basic understanding of energy, its relationship to man's basic needs, and the importance of applying conservation measures in everyday life.

Major topics include kinds and forms of power, sources of energy, kinds of energy, environmental terms, basic electricity, simple machines and their applications, pollution, and proper understanding of energy and its relationship to light and sound.

Again, emphasis is placed on vocabulary development, reading comprehension and inference skills, decoding skills, basic concepts of energy, and modern developments in this field.

The students will demonstrate perceptual skills, as well as alphabetization ability. This important unit presents several challenges to the students and will motivate them to do further research on some of the topics presented.

Each of the activities poses a challenge. The students will demonstrate their eagerness to find the answer, and thereby increase their knowledge about the concepts presented in this section.

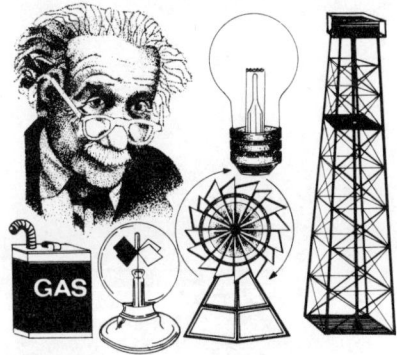

KINDS OF POWER

Work is done by using some kind of power. There are many kinds of power that are used to perform work. The earliest form of power was *man*. Then man learned to train animals to work for him and *animal power* was used whenever possible. Man then learned to harness the wind, and *wind power* was used to move ships and turn wheels. Man then discovered water as a cheap source of power, and *water power* was put to work.

With the invention of the internal combustion engine which burns gas or oil, *engine power* became more efficient and cheaper. Engine power also includes steam power, atomic power, and electric power. Modern civilization has developed because of these many sources of power.

In the chart below, list five items for each kind of power. (Example: *Animal*—dog power, used by Eskimos)

	Wind	*Gas/Oil*	*Water*	*Electric*	*Animal*
1.					
2.					
3.					
4.					
5.					

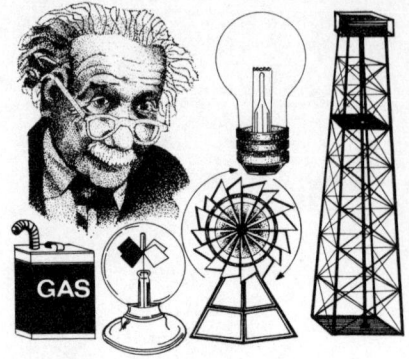

FORMS OF POWER

Power comes in many different forms. For this exercise, you will be thinking of the many different forms of power and their uses.

1. Name five things that use *wind* for power (Example: kite):

   a. _____
   b. _____
   c. _____
   d. _____
   e. _____

2. Name five things that use *fuel* for power (Example: motorcycle):

   a. _____
   b. _____
   c. _____
   d. _____
   e. _____

3. Name five things that use *electricity* for power (Example: television set):

   a. _____
   b. _____
   c. _____
   d. _____
   e. _____

4. Name three new things that use the *sun* as a source of power (Example: solar watch):

   a. _____
   b. _____
   c. _____

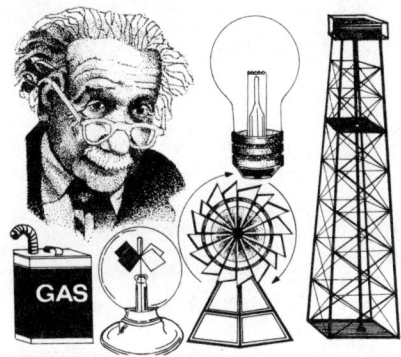

KINDS OF ENERGY

Energy is the ability to do work, and it is divided into two different classifications.

Kinetic energy comes from some type of motion. Movement is always present in kinetic energy forms. If you roll a bowling ball at some pins, the rolling ball has kinetic energy. Water flowing over a dam is also a form of kinetic energy.

Potential energy is energy that is stored in an object. There is no movement in potential energy unless force is applied in some form. A dry cell is one form of potential energy. Once we hook up wires to it, we can use the stored-up energy inside it. Something has to happen to the container of potential energy in order for it to be activated.

1. Look at each item below. Write whether you think it is kinetic (k) or potential (p) energy:

a. kerosene _____   e. uranium _____
b. a glass of water _____   f. wood _____
c. football in flight _____   g. a speeding bullet _____
d. coal _____   h. fire _____

2. Match the type of energy with its source, from the list below:

a. Mechanical energy comes from _____
b. Heat energy comes from _____
c. Wave energy comes from _____
d. Electrical energy comes from _____
e. Chemical energy comes from _____
f. Nuclear energy comes from _____

a flow of electrons   machines
the sun   fast moving molecules
splitting the atom   storage battery

Conservation and Energy

- -

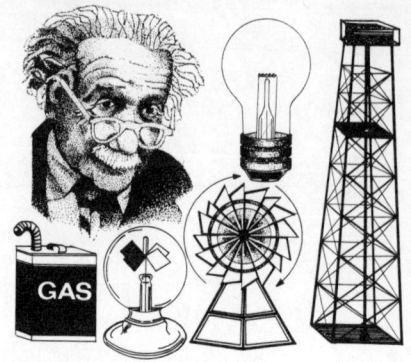

USING MOTOR ENERGY IN THE HOME

Many appliances in your home are connected to motors that use energy. For instance, a fan uses electrical energy operating a motor. A washing machine also uses a motor.

1. Make a list of at least 12 things in your house which may be operated by a motor:

   a. _____   g. _____
   b. _____   h. _____
   c. _____   i. _____
   d. _____   j. _____
   e. _____   k. _____
   f. _____   l. _____

2. List 6 things in your garage or outside the home which may be operated by a motor (Example: electric saw):

   a. _____   d. _____
   b. _____   e. _____
   c. _____   f. _____

3. List several things you might have that operate by a *spring motor*. One example would be a watch.

   a. _____
   b. _____
   c. _____

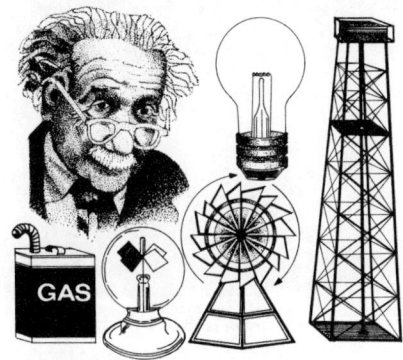

TRANSPORTATION CLASSIFICATION

Information can be organized and arranged in logical groups to help you understand it more easily. This process is called *classification*.

In the exercises below, classify the methods of transportation under the various categories listed.

glider	spaceship	roller skates	jet
bicycle	rowboat	skateboard	canoe
blimp	airplane	motorbike	helicopter
rocket	kayak	escalator	covered wagon

Fuel Power	*Human Power*	*Animal Power*
_____	_____	_____
_____	_____	_____
_____	_____	_____
_____	_____	_____
_____	_____	_____

Now, classify those transportation methods that fit these categories:

Land	*Air*	*Water*
_____	_____	_____
_____	_____	_____
_____	_____	_____
_____	_____	_____

Conservation and Energy   155

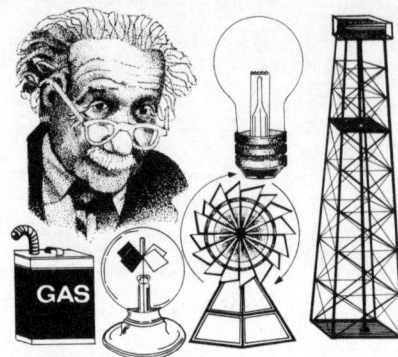

UNDERSTANDING ENVIRONMENTAL TERMS

Many terms being used today are connected with our environment. Try to match the terms in Column A with their definitions in Column B. If there are some you do not know, use your dictionary to discover the right answer.

Column A

_____ 1. pollution
_____ 2. recycling
_____ 3. ecology
_____ 4. environment
_____ 5. smog
_____ 6. soil erosion
_____ 7. sanitary landfill
_____ 8. natural resources
_____ 9. effluent
_____10. decibel
_____11. insecticide
_____12. habitat
_____13. solid waste
_____14. hydrosphere

Column B

a. the world around us

b. things supplied by Nature, such as coal, trees, and oil

c. the water world, including oceans, lakes, and rivers

d. a unit of measure of noise

e. the relationships between living things, their surroundings, and each other

f. contamination of the air, land, and water of our environment

g. discarded trash, including glass, garbage, cans, and paper

h. air containing smoke and fog

i. loss of soil by the action of wind and water

j. the natural home of an animal species or individual

k. the release of waste products by a factory process or system

l. poison to kill insects

m. a planned area where garbage and trash are buried

n. the reuse of materials and resources

Conservation and Energy

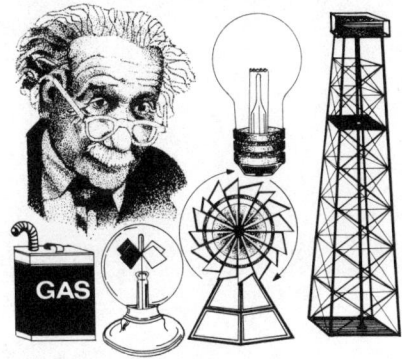

UNDERSTANDING ENERGY TERMS

Do you know that the word *energy* is becoming a household term? There are many words related to energy. How many of these do you know or have you heard?

Match the energy terms in Column A with their proper definitions in Column B. Remember, if you need help consult your dictionary.

Column A

_____ 1. anything that is burned or consumed to produce energy

_____ 2. the ability to do work.

_____ 3. heat from the earth

_____ 4. something that makes work easier

_____ 5. a flow of electrical particles along a wire or conductor

_____ 6. a machine that takes electrical energy and converts it into mechanical energy

_____ 7. a combination of basic machines that converts fuel into energy and motion

_____ 8. the measure of the amount of work that can be done in a specific unit of time

_____ 9. a machine that takes mechanical energy and changes it into electrical energy

_____ 10. the use of water in making electricity

_____ 11. a small unit of matter

_____ 12. energy gathered and converted from the sun

Column B

a. solar energy

b. machine

c. engine

d. generator

e. atom

f. electricity

g. energy

h. fuel

i. power

j. motor

k. hydroelectric

l. geothermal

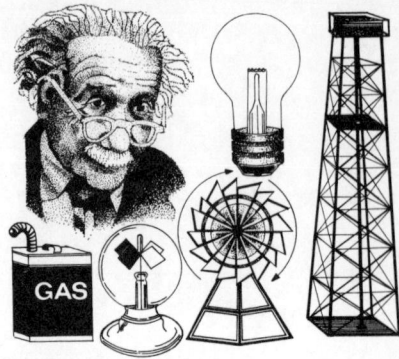

LIGHT AND ITS SOURCES

There are two types of light sources. The first type is *natural light*. This includes light from the sun (which is really burning gases), light from the moon (which is reflected light from the sun), and light that comes from fireflies and some deep sea fish.

The second type of light source is *artificial light*. The word *artificial* means not real, but an imitation. Therefore, light that comes from a candle is artificial light, as it comes from a man-made object.

1. List some sources of artificial light that you are now familiar with:

   a. _____ d. _____

   b. _____ e. _____

   c. _____ f. _____

2. For the following objects, list whether the light is artificial (a) or natural (n):

   a. star _____   f. battery light _____

   b. gas burner _____   g. match light _____

   c. lightning _____   h. meteor _____

   d. neon bulb _____   i. wood burning _____

   e. comet _____   j. rainbow _____

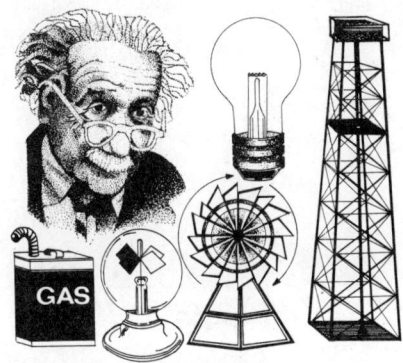

NAME	DATE
GRADE	TEACHER

ELECTRICITY

Just about everyone in the United States now uses electricity. Not too long ago, there were some homes that did not burn electricity. However, because we depend on electricity to power so many appliances, it has become very widely used.

1. Can you define *electricity*?

_____

_____

2. Is lightning a form of electricity? If yes, explain why:

_____

_____

3. Is electricity formed by connecting batteries together? How?

_____

_____

4. What is meant by *static electricity*? (Use your dictionary.)

_____

_____

5. What fuels are used to make electricity?

    a. _____
    b. _____
    c. _____

6. List eight items you see every day that use electricity:

    a. _____   e. _____
    b. _____   f. _____
    c. _____   g. _____
    d. _____   h. _____

Conservation and Energy

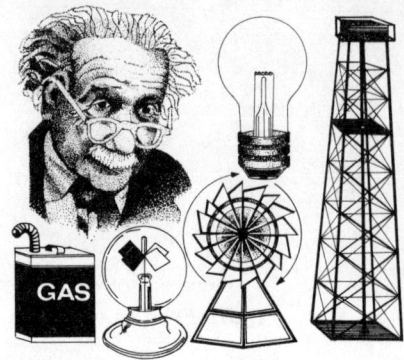

SIMPLE MACHINES

There are six simple machines that help man to do work more easily. The simple machines are:

pulley	wheel/axle	wedge
lever	screw	inclined plane

In the puzzle below, put the name of the simple machine that helps this tool or invention to move easily.

1. conveyer _____
2. bicycle _____
3. winch _____
4. crowbar _____
5. watch _____
6. automobile jack _____
7. ramp _____
8. axe _____
9. shovel _____
10. motor _____
11. chisel _____
12. hoist _____
13. bolt _____
14. elevator _____
15. automobile _____

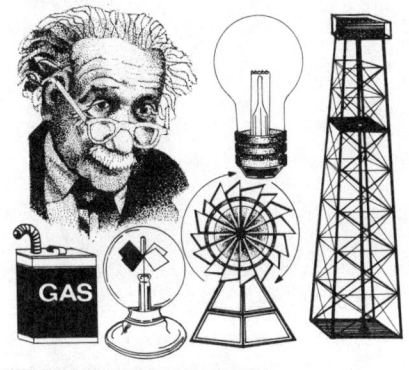

POLLUTION—A MODERN PROBLEM

The *biosphere* is where all living things exist, including all plants and animals. Each area of the biosphere has its own environment, and this environment includes climate, plant life, animal life, bodies of water, and soil. All parts of the environment affect other parts and any change in conditions causes problems.

One of the modern problems affecting our biosphere is *pollution*. Pollution refers to the impurity and uncleanliness of the environment. The scientific word for this is *contamination*. Contamination of the environment comes mainly from certain chemical gases produced by man.

A major source of pollution is the burning of materials. These materials are called *hydrocarbons* because what is burned consists of hydrogen and carbon. Coal, oil, and gas are forms of hydrocarbons that are part of fossil fuels. Most nations of the world burn hydrocarbons as a form of energy and the result is pollution.

Carbon monoxide, which is the exhaust of a car, is not only poisonous and deadly, but it also pollutes the atmosphere. *Sulfur*, which comes from burning fuel, is another contaminant of the atmosphere. *Carbon dioxide* is another pollutant. *Smog* is a form of pollution caused by a mixing of gases and the sun's rays. Smog can also kill people. *Aerosol* cans, which contain tiny liquid particles of material, are also forms of pollution. All of these things make the air we breathe impure.

Congress passed a Clean Air Act in 1970 which ordered factories to reduce air and water pollution. Air is a precious resource which we need for survival.

1. Define *pollution*:

_____

_____

2. List some things that pollute our air:

a. _____

b. _____

c. _____

d. _____

3. What is the *biosphere?*

_____

_____

4. What is another name for car exhaust?

_____

5. Why is smog dangerous?

_____

_____

6. How is smog formed?

_____

_____

7. What does the Clean Air Act of 1970 do?

_____

_____

8. What are *hydrocarbons?*

_____

_____

9. Make as many words as you can from the letters in P O L L U T I O N:

_____

_____

_____

Conservation and Energy

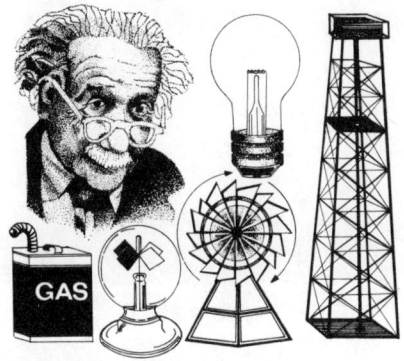

CONSERVING HOME ENERGY

Read each of the statements below. Then, in one or two words, write what you could do to conserve energy for that particular item.

1. A dripping faucet _____
2. An open window with heat on _____
3. Draft around a closed door _____
4. Throwing out plastic containers _____
5. Lights left on _____
6. Oversized light bulbs _____
7. Television left on _____
8. An empty refrigerator _____
9. Freezer door left open _____
10. Wasting ice cubes _____
11. Buying cans with dents in them _____
12. Throwing out paper bags _____
13. Overuse of water _____
14. Overcooking of foods _____
15. Broken and cracked windows _____

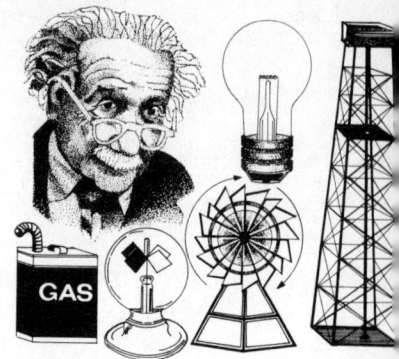

HOUSEHOLD TOOLS

Can you find some common household tools in this puzzle?

```
H  A  W  L  Y  V  I  S  E  K  A  N  S  T  L  I  O
S  A  W  I  C  O  M  P  A  S  S  T  L  O  B  H  V
S  O  M  S  S  L  E  V  E  L  F  K  C  O  L  C  N
L  K  J  M  P  L  A  N  E  B  M  U  L  P  A  N  A
E  R  U  L  E  I  F  S  G  L  U  E  S  D  A  U  I
I  O  T  D  W  R  E  N  C  H  S  U  R  B  S  P  L
D  R  I  L  L  D  S  C  R  E  W  D  R  I  V  E  R
S  A  B  E  F  I  N  K  C  L  A  M  P  S  F  D  S
```

hammer	drill	saw	awl
wrench	level	plane	rule
vise	nail	compass	screwdriver
die	brush	lock	clamp
plumb	punch	glue	knife
oil	bolts	bit	

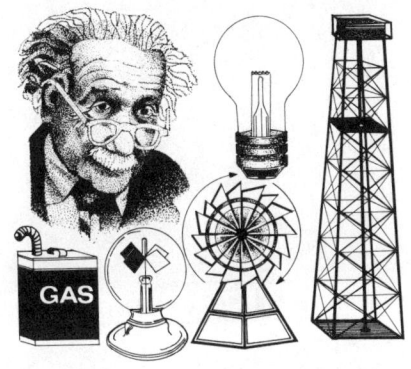

A HOME FOR GARBAGE

Even garbage has a home. What used to be called a "dump" is now called a *sanitary landfill*. A landfill is a planned area where trash, garbage, and other waste materials are buried. There are very strict laws governing how a landfill is managed. Every community must use some sort of a landfill site.

Think about the following questions, which are all related to landfills, and write your answers as completely as possible:

1. Why must every community have a sanitary landfill?

   _____

   _____

2. Why does the size of the landfill depend on the size of the community?

   _____

   _____

3. What other factors, besides community size, would determine the size of a landfill?

   _____

   _____

4. Look up the word *refuse* in your dictionary. Write its definition and state how it refers to landfill:

   _____

   _____

5. Find out how garbage in your community is collected. Who does it, the city or private agencies? How often is it collected? Where is the landfill in your community?

   _____

   _____

   _____

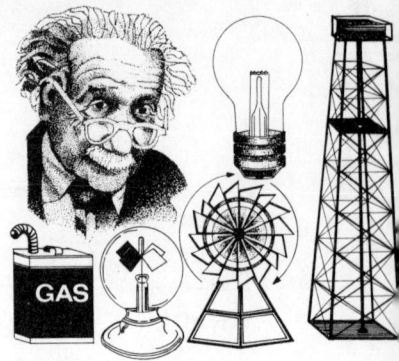

LIGHT AS ENERGY

Light is really a form of energy. Light consists of tiny units called *photons* moving in all directions from where the light starts or *originates*. Light travels in a wave and is called a *light wave*. When light waves travel, they go in all directions. Light travels very rapidly. In fact, light travels *186,000 miles per second*. This is known as the *speed of light*.

Light can bounce back from objects, too. The bouncing of light from an object is called *reflection*. The smoother the surface, the better the reflection will be. Therefore, light bounces off a white wall better than a brick wall because the white wall is smoother and can reflect more light because of its lighter color.

Light can also be bent. The bending of light is called *refraction*. Do not confuse refraction with reflection. There is a very strong difference. We can bend light by having it go through a piece of glass that is shaped like a triangle. This triangle of glass is called a *prism*. When light is bent (refracted) through a prism, we get the colors of the rainbow. This is called a *spectrum*. The spectrum colors are red, orange, yellow, green, blue, indigo, and violet, in that order.

1. What is *reflection* of light?

_____

_____

2. How fast does light travel?

_____

_____

3. What is light?

_____

_____

4. When light travels, it is called a _____.

5. What is *refraction* of light?

_____

_____

6. A triangular piece of glass used to refract light is called a

_____ .

7. What does *originate* mean?

_____

_____

8. Look up these terms in your dictionary and write a definition
   for each one:

   shadow   _____

   spectrum   _____

   illuminate _____

9. Look up the word *light* in an encyclopedia. Write down a few
   facts that you have read:

   _____

   _____

   _____

   _____

10. Why does light bounce or reflect better off a smooth object?

   _____

   _____

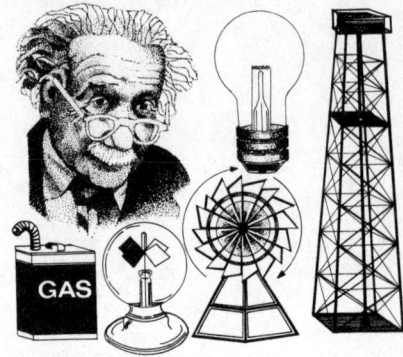

THE SCIENCE OF SOUND

Sound is produced when vibrations (sound waves) pass through the air. A telephone bell, a violin, a hammer, and tapping your toes all produce some type of sound. Air must be present for sound to be heard. There is no sound in a *vacuum*, which is the absence of air. The loudness or softness of sound is measured by a unit called a *decibel*. As the sound gets louder, higher decibels are registered.

Surprisingly, sound travels at about 740 miles per hour. This is known as the limit of the *sound barrier*. It is also known as *Mach I*. An airplane breaking the sound barrier is flying faster than the speed of sound, or 740 miles per hour. That is why you hear the noise after the airplane passes.

Human beings can hear from 16 to 16,000 vibrations per second. Dogs have very excellent hearing and can hear *ultrasonic* sounds which humans cannot hear.

Sound Decibel Chart

heartbeat	10 decibels	street traffic	80 decibels
whisper	20 decibels	car horn	90 decibels
typewriter	40 decibels	screaming	100 decibels
talking	60 decibels	thunder	110 decibels
barking dog	70 decibels	painful sounds	130 decibels

Look at each of the sounds listed below. Determine the number of decibels you think would apply to each. Check the chart above to guide you.

1. a light switch being clicked on   _____ decibels
2. crash of a cymbal   _____ decibels
3. telephone bell   _____ decibels
4. radio announcer   _____ decibels
5. music from a radio   _____ decibels
6. loud yelling   _____ decibels

7. pencil breaking   _____ decibels
8. police whistle   _____ decibels
9. a glass breaking   _____ decibels
10. turning a page in a book   _____ decibels
11. book falling to the floor   _____ decibels
12. winding your watch   _____ decibels

Fill in each of the following definitions in your own words:

      a. A *decibel* is   _____.
      b. *Vacuum* means   _____.
      c. The *speed of sound* is   _____.
      d. *Vibrations* are   _____.
      e. *Mach 2* would be   _____.
      f. *Mach 3* would be   _____.

(Do you know that the United States has airplanes that fly Mach 3?)

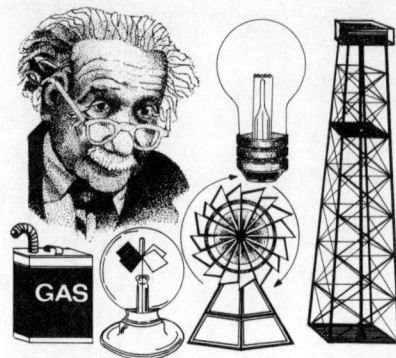

CONSERVATION AND ENERGY MYSTERY PUZZLE

Unscramble the letters for each clue and make a word out of the circled letters.

1. does work for man   C H I M E A N

2. the beginning   S C O U R E

3. they grow   S T P N A L

4. old, dead plants and   S L I F O S S
   animals

5. used to do work   R E W P O

Circled word is _____.

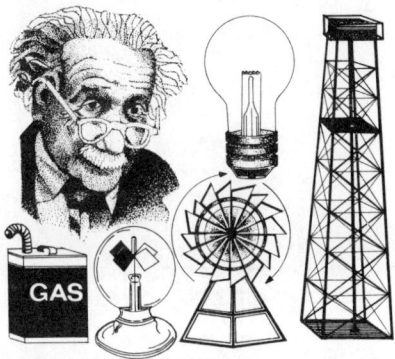

CONSERVATION AND ENERGY ALPHABETIZED WORDS

Write a word related to conservation and energy that begins with each letter listed. Think carefully.

A _____

B _____

C _____

D _____

E _____

F _____

G _____

H _____

K _*kinetic*_____

L _____

M _____

N _____

P _____

R _____

S _____

T _____

W _____

CONSERVATION AND ENERGY WORD FUN

Find each of the words below in this letter jumble.

```
G A S O P U W W U
T E C E M F E E E
N A O L W I N D L
E Z N L S O E E E
M Y S E O A R N C
N B E C I G G I T
O L R S L A Y L R
R I V E R L I O I
I G A R A L O S C
V H T R A E S A I
N T I F U E L G T
E P O W E R T S Y
B V N R O T O M F
```

oil	energy	fuel	dew
electricity	wind	gas	power
geology	motor	environment	earth
light	cell	river	gasoline
conservation	eyes	soil	solar

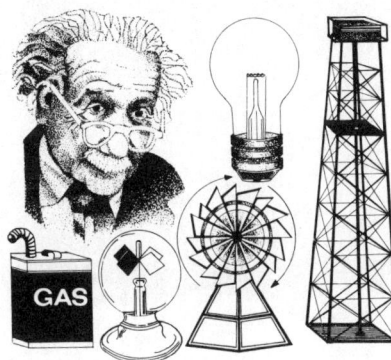

CONSERVATION SCRAMBLED TERMS

Each of these terms has been discussed in this chapter. A very brief definition is given to you. Write the correct word next to the definition.

1. tityleecric _____ a form of current
2. wepor _____ a form of energy
3. rgeyen _____ what makes things go
4. yaibtah _____ home for animals
5. lufe _____ source of power
6. moats _____ smallest particles known
7. nikecit _____ form of energy
8. chineam _____ object that does work
9. cideebl _____ measures sound
10. fanldlil _____ storage area
11. tomro _____ an engine
12. pohesrrewo _____ measures amount of work
13. tighnling _____ atmospheric electricity
14. taconesrvnoi _____ saving things
15. tairifclai _____ not natural

MATTER

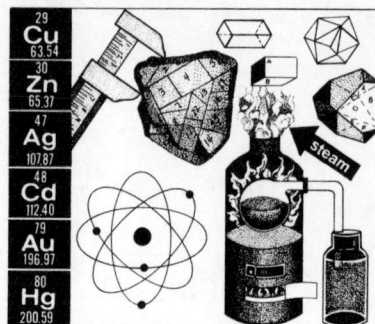

INTRODUCTION TO THE TEACHER

The subject of matter is generally covered in most elementary school science units. This section provides a basic understanding of the physical and chemical properties of matter. It presents terminology on rocks, earth minerals, and the basic state of matter.

This short chapter is designed to build a more comprehensive understanding of matter and its relationships to industrial uses. Again, reading comprehension skills, inference skills, and decoding skills are a priority. The students will learn about the basic types of rocks and their uses in modern science.

A brief presentation on atoms and rocks will build the students' basic understanding in addition to their regular textbook assignments. Some mathematical calculations are included to test reasoning and observation powers.

Each drill activity and puzzle challenge has been designed to build an awareness of the science concepts described in this chapter.

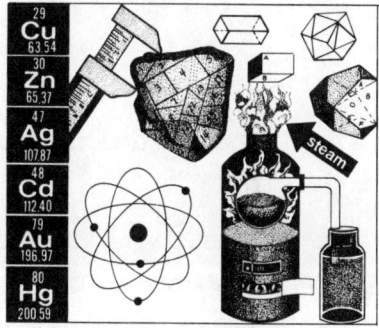

UNDERSTANDING MATTER

Matter is anything that takes up space and has weight. Matter can be invisible as well as visible. Matter is found in three separate forms, sometimes called *states*. Matter can be a *solid*, like coal, wood, or your shoes. Matter can be a *liquid*, such as milk, gasoline, or water. Matter can also be a *gas*, such as air (a combination of gases), helium, or oxygen.

Solid matter has a definite size and shape.

Liquid matter has a definite size and has the shape of the container it is in.

Gas matter has no definite size. It also takes the shape of the container it is in.

Listed below are some forms of matter. List each under its proper form or state. Reread the information in the first paragraph if you have any problems.

desk	hydrogen	pencil	oil
pen	vinegar	ruler	cough syrup
air	sock	clock	automobile
atom	tree	steam	carpet

Solid	*Liquid*	*Gas*
_____	_____	_____
_____	_____	_____
_____	_____	_____
_____	_____	_____
_____	_____	_____

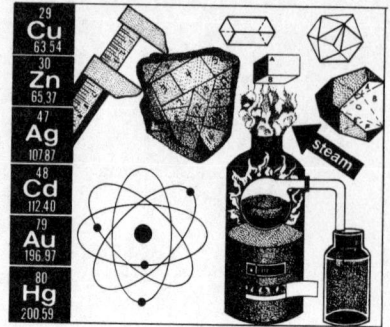

CHANGING MATTER

1. Look at the items listed below and then change each into another form of the same physical matter:

   a. oranges _____
   b. potatoes _____
   c. trees _____
   d. water vapor _____
   e. boards _____
   f. steel _____
   g. glass _____
   h. milk _____

   Why do you think it is easy to recognize a physical change?
   _____

2. List below some items that you can see that have undergone some type of physical change:

   from _____ to _____
   from _____ to _____
   from _____ to _____
   from _____ to _____

- -

PHYSICAL PROPERTIES OF MATTER

If matter is something that takes up space and has weight, then we can tell something about it by using our senses of touch and sight. By touching and seeing, we can determine the *physical properties* of matter. We can tell the weight, color, texture, hardness, softness, and size of matter.

Which physical property would you associate with each of the following forms of matter? (Some may have two properties.)

a. glass _____ h. silk _____
b. lead _____ i. sandstone _____
c. iron _____ j. emerald _____
d. copper _____ k. water _____
e. ruby _____ l. oil _____
f. aluminum _____ m. diamond _____
g. bark of a tree _____ n. wool _____

Matter also has *chemical properties*. If you were to light a candle, it would give off heat and light. Those are chemical properties of a candle.

1. What would happen if you left a nail out in wet weather for a few weeks?

_____

_____

2. Which metal would not be affected by wet weather if it was left out for a long period of time?

_____

3. Name a chemical property change that you are familiar with:

_____

Matter   177

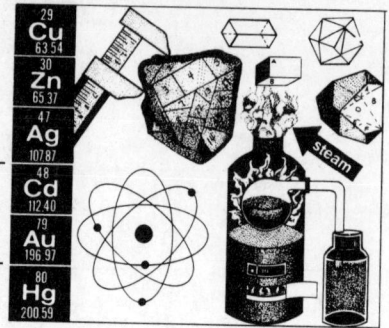

Connect the dots and find this form of matter.

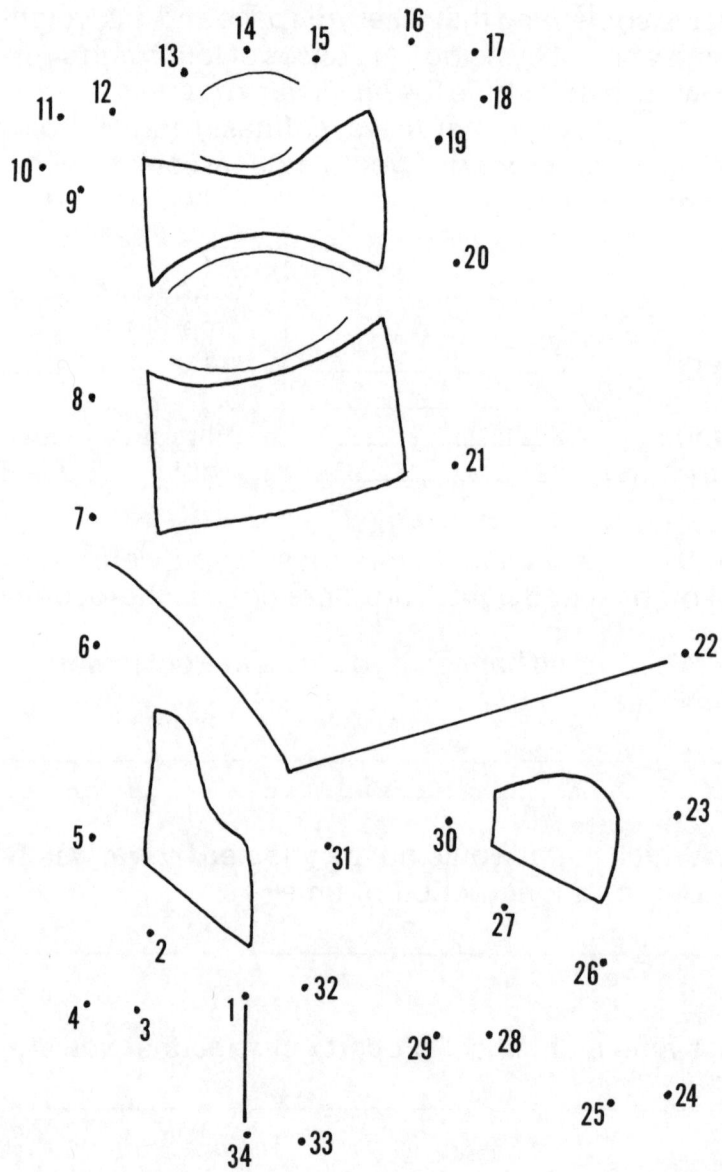

14
15
16
13
17
11
12
18
10
19
9
8
7
6
22
5
31
30
23
2
27
32
26
4
3
1
29
28
34
33
25
24

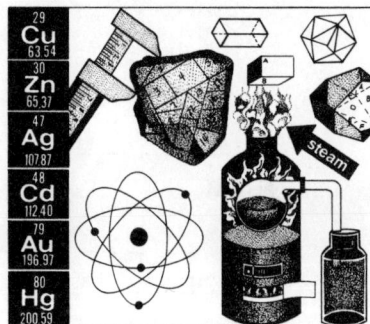

CHEMICAL SYMBOLS AND MATTER

Chemistry is the study of the composition of matter. The scientists who study chemistry (*chemists*) have a special code for all of the elements which make up matter. Perhaps you are familiar with some of the following symbols:

H—Hydrogen	I—Iodine
O—Oxygen	Na—Sodium (salt)
Fe—Iron	S—Sulfur (on the tip of a match)
K—Potassium	Cl—Chlorine (used in swimming pools)
Zn—Zinc	C—Carbon (burnt ashes)

If we combine two or more elements of matter, we get a new symbol. H_2O is water: 1 part Hydrogen and 2 parts Oxygen.

Write the names of the elements of matter next to the symbols:

1. CO_2 _____ and _____ (carbon dioxide, what you exhale)

2. $C_{12}H_{22}O_{11}$ _____ and _____ and _____ (sugar)

3. H_2O_2 _____ and _____ (hydrogen peroxide, used for minor cuts)

4. Fe_2O_3 _____ and _____ (rust)

5. H_2SO_4 _____ and _____ and _____ (sulfuric acid)

Matter

MOON WEIGHT

Matter, we learned before, takes up space and has weight. The amount of matter that an object contains is called *mass*. On the moon, the pull of gravity on an object is much less than on the same object on earth. For example, a 6-pound object on the earth would weigh only 1 pound on the moon. A 12-pound object on earth would weigh 2 pounds on the moon.

The weight of anything on the moon is $\frac{1}{6}$ the weight of the same object on earth. Knowing this, we can figure out moon and earth weights.

Fill in the correct weights for each person on the chart below:

	Earth Weight	Moon Weight
Bob:	144 pounds	_____
Alice:	_____	20 pounds
Bill:	_____	15 pounds
Mary:	_____	24 pounds
Hattie:	180 pounds	_____
Scott:	_____	12 pounds
Luann:	126 pounds	_____

Find out your weight. How much would you weigh on the moon?

_____

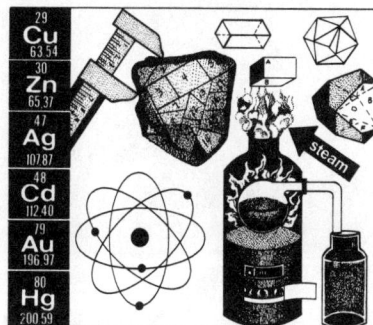

ATOMS

An *atom* is the smallest particle of matter. Atoms are so small that they cannot be seen and they come in different shapes. An atom has a center called a *nucleus*. Inside the nucleus are two types of particles, *protons* and *neutrons*. Outside the nucleus, moving in orbits around it, are other particles called *electrons*. Electrons have a negative electrical charge. Protons have a positive charge. Neutrons, as you might guess from their name, are neutral and have no electrical charge.

A *molecule* is a form of matter that is made up of two or more atoms. Molecules are found in all things. A molecule is the smallest particle of a substance that has all of the properties of that particular substance. Molecules are always moving. They strike other molecules and bounce off in different directions. In things that are solid, like a pencil or a chair, the molecules are very close together. In liquids, molecules are further apart. In gases, the molecules are very far apart and don't bounce into each other as much.

An *element* is a substance that is made up of only one kind of atom. Gold, silver, oxygen, iron, and copper are all examples of elements. There are 106 known elements in our universe. There may even be elements we have not discovered yet!

A *compound* is a substance that is made up of two or more elements. Just as compound words consists of two or more words, so do compounds in science contain two or more separate elements. Water is a compound because it consists of hydrogen (2 parts) and oxygen (1 part). The symbol for water is H_2O. Compounds can be separated into elements by using some form of energy.

1. List the two parts of an atom: _____ and _____ .

2. The part of an atom that is positively charged is the _____ .

3. An *element* is:

_____

4. List six more elements that did not appear in the paragraphs above:

    a. _____   d. _____

    b. _____   e. _____

    c. _____   f. _____

5. Something that is made up of two or more atoms is called a _____ .

6. List some facts about molecules:

    a. _____

    b. _____

    c. _____

7. Describe a *compound*:

_____

_____

8. The center of an atom is called _____ .

9. What is the symbol for water? _____ .

10. Why is water considered a compound?

_____

_____

11. How many known elements are there at this time? _____ .

12. Gas molecules are very _____ .

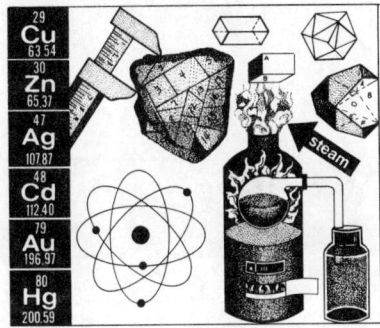

NAME	DATE
GRADE	TEACHER

WET OR DRY?

The words below all describe places on the earth that are either wet or dry. Place each word under the proper heading of Wet or Dry. If you do not know a word, look it up in your dictionary.

harbor	bay	gorge	inlet
gulf	pampas	strait	peninsula
canal	plain	marsh	lagoon
reservoir	isthmus	oasis	cliff
lowland	sea	wave	island
canyon	delta	tide	plateau
pond			

Wet   *Dry*

_____   _____
_____   _____
_____   _____
_____   _____
_____   _____
_____   _____
_____   _____
_____   _____
_____   _____
_____   _____

Matter

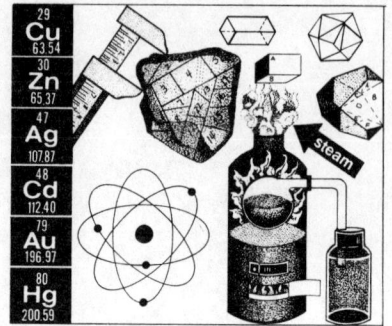

ROCKS

Rocks are minerals. There are many different kinds of rocks, which can be classified into three main types: *sedimentary* rocks, *igneous* rocks, and *metamorphic* rocks.

Sedimentary rocks are the most common type of rock found on our planet. They cover about 75 percent of the earth's surface. A sedimentary rock is formed from parts of *sediment*, which are particles that have settled at the bottom of a liquid. Rocks are broken into smaller particles and are carried by wind and water. A common type of sedimentary rock is *sandstone*. Another common type is *shale*. Shale is made of thin layers of clay.

Igneous rocks are formed by heat and pressure. The liquid magma from the deep parts of the earth melt and grind together and a hard rock is formed. Igneous is a word which means *fire*. One example of igneous rock is the *lava* that is thrown out of a volcano by heat and pressure. It cools quickly upon hitting the surface of the earth. Granite, quartz, and mica are also forms of igneous rock.

Metamorphic rocks have undergone some type of change. Metamorphic means *change*. Most metamorphic rocks are formed from the basic sedimentary rock, but they are not as hard as igneous rocks. Metamorphic rocks are made deep in the earth. Marble, slate, and quartzite are forms of metamorphic rock.

1. List the three basic types of rocks:

   a. _____
   b. _____
   c. _____

2. What does *igneous* mean?

   _____
   _____

3. What does *metamorphic* mean?

_____

_____

4. What kind of a rock is *lava*?

_____

5. List some rocks that are igneous:

_____

_____

6. List some sedimentary rocks:

_____

_____

7. List some metamorphic rocks:

_____

_____

8. What does the word *sediment* mean?

_____

_____

9. Look in your science book or dictionary and list what is made from the following rocks:

    marble   _____

    sandstone   _____

    slate   _____

    granite   _____

10. How many words can you make from the letters in the word SANDSTONE?

_____

_____

_____

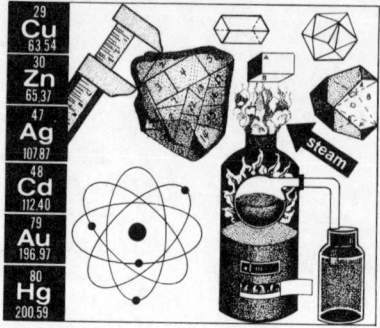

ROCK USES

Rocks can be used for many purposes. Think of some ways that rocks can be used and list them here. For example, some rocks are used for decoration, such as in an arrangement in a flower garden or a flower pot. Can you think of at least eight more uses of rocks?

1. _____
2. _____
3. _____
4. _____
5. _____
6. _____
7. _____
8. _____

List eight different uses of metals. List the particular metal and what it is used for. (Example: copper used for making pennies.)

1. _____ used for _____
2. _____ used for _____
3. _____ used for _____
4. _____ used for _____
5. _____ used for _____
6. _____ used for _____
7. _____ used for _____
8. _____ used for _____

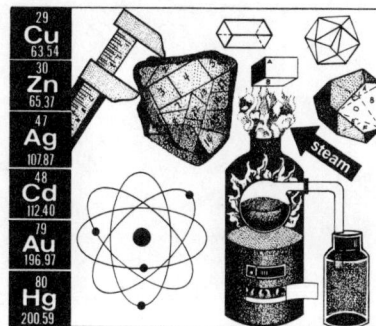

MINERAL MATTER OF THE EARTH

The outer crust of the earth near the surface is called the *lithosphere*. This word comes from the Greek *lithos* which means rock or stone, and *sphere* meaning round. The ground on which you walk is composed of dirt and hard rock, or soil. All of these things are types of matter from which the earth was originally formed.

Rocks can be single minerals or combinations of minerals. *Minerals* are a special kind of matter. Minerals are always solid, they are formed in nature, and they are *inorganic*, or without life. Minerals are also always composed in the same way.

Minerals can be recognized in many ways. You can recognize minerals by their appearance. You can also feel, smell, and taste minerals. A mineral can be shiny, like gold, silver, and lead. A mineral can be tested for hardness. A hard mineral always scratches a softer mineral. Diamonds, the hardest mineral known, will scratch every other mineral. Minerals have color, and this is another way of identifying them. Semiprecious stones are identified by their color as well as their hardness. Sulphur, which is the material at the end of a matchstick, is usually yellow in appearance. Copper has a dark reddish appearance.

Rocks are made up of either single minerals or combinations of minerals. Rock was once underneath the crust of the earth. When the rock was in liquid form, called *magma*, it moved toward the surface of the earth and then hardened to form many large rocks.

1. What is a *mineral?*

   _____

   _____

2. The outer crust of the earth is called the _____ .

3. *Magma* is a type of _____ rock.

4. What are some properties of minerals?

    a. _____

    b. _____

    c. _____

5. What is the hardest mineral known?

_____

6. *Without life* can be described by the word _____ .

7. What are some ways you can test minerals?

_____

_____

8. What mineral is used in making matches?

_____

9. Is a rock a mineral?

_____

10. See how many words you can make from the letters in the word M I N E R A L:

_____

_____

_____

11. How did rock get to the surface of the earth?

_____

_____

12. Can a rock have more than one mineral in it?

_____

13. What does the word *sphere* mean?

_____

_____

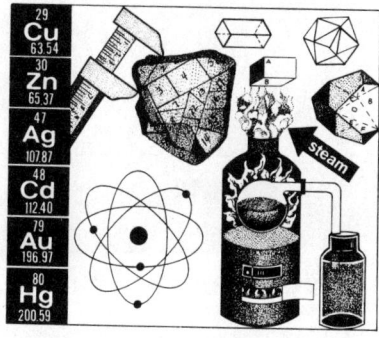

MATTER MYSTERY PUZZLE

Each of these matter words should now be familiar to you. Unscramble the letters and then write the word spelled from the circled letters.

1. small, invisible things   M   O   A   T   S

2. found all over   S   C   O   K   R

3. very hard   L   I   D   O   S

4. 75 percent of earth's surface   T   R   A   W   E

5. a source of power   G   E   R   N   Y   E

6. top of earth's surface   S   T   R   C   U

7. to bounce back   F   E   R   C   E   T   L

Circled word is _____ .

Matter

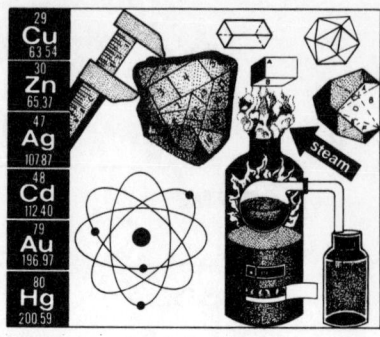

MATTER ALPHABETIZED WORDS

Write one word related to matter that begins with each letter listed below:

A _____

B _____

C _____

D _____

E _____

F _____

G _____

H _____

I _____

L _____

M _____

N _____

O _____

P _____

R _____

S _____

T _____

W *weight* _____

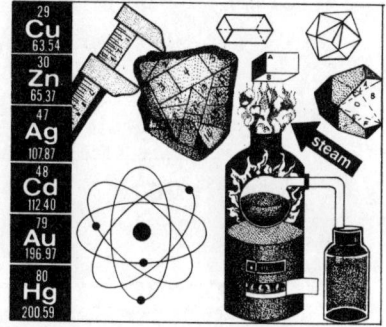

MATTER WORD FUN

The words you have to find in this puzzle all have to do with the topic of matter. Can you locate all of these words within ten minutes?

```
A  E  L  S  D  R  I  T  R  A  C  Y
S  X  A  I  W  E  R  C  S  A  H  E
J  A  L  I  O  V  W  E  D  G  E  N
P  O  G  X  R  E  T  T  A  M  M  I
S  Y  M  B  O  L  Q  N  O  R  I  C
M  D  O  O  W  E  G  N  A  H  C  I
E  L  M  A  C  H  I  N  E  S  A  D
G  T  G  O  L  D  I  U  Q  I  L  E
B  L  A  C  I  S  Y  H  P  O  O  M
A  P  U  L  L  E  Y  E  N  A  L  P
L  A  I  R  E  T  A  M  B  L  U  E
```

blue	cart	material	gold
lever	wedge	chemical	matter
air	change	iron	oil
gems	axe	medicine	physical
liquid	machine	plane	pulley
symbol	gas	wood	screw

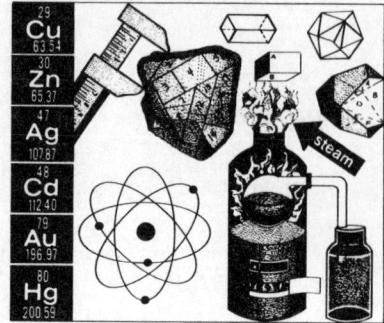

MATTER SCRAMBLED TERMS

Now that you have learned about matter and its properties, unscramble these words related to it. Check each definition first.

1. velre   _____   a basic machine
2. geoxyn   _____   pure gas necessary for life
3. demciien   _____   used to cure people
4. barcon   _____   burned material
5. barhro   _____   port for ships
6. perocp   _____   reddish metal
7. tamret   _____   material around us
8. deweg   _____   simple machine to split things
9. vilser   _____   used in making coins
10. quilid   _____   fluid material
11. hisycalp   _____   something tangible
12. gheiwt   _____   you measure this
13. madinod   _____   hardest mineral known
14. lupley   _____   used to lift things
15. pasirni   _____   mild medication
16. losdi   _____   hard, dense, having shape

COMBINED ACTIVITIES

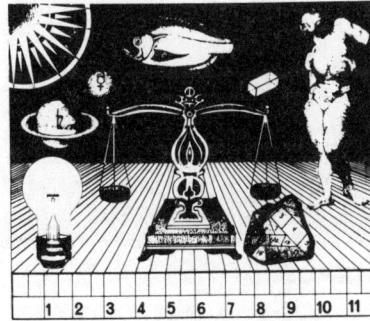

INTRODUCTION TO THE TEACHER

A large variety of exercises is provided in this chapter which covers all of the chapter headings in the book. Each activity is different and is designed to further strengthen all of the skills already discussed in the previous chapters.

You may want to relate the activities to the appropriate chapter as you study each topic, or you may want to use the activities as a follow-up exercise with a separate identity.

The activities can be selected randomly or used as they are presented here.

All of the skills discussed as basic for learning in this book are covered here. As the children do these exercises, they should demonstrate a quicker ability to solve puzzles and answer questions. Of special importance are the science words relating to each alphabet letter. Students can employ dictionary skills to solve these challenging games.

8

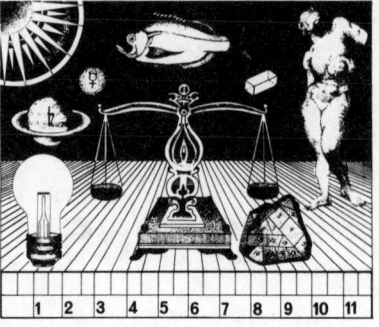

FINDING SCIENCE WORDS WITH "A"

Each of the definitions below can be answered with a science-related word beginning with A. Study each clue carefully and then write the correct word.

1. part of the body that expands _____
2. a frame with sliding beads for counting _____
3. surrounds the earth _____
4. a dull, steady pain _____
5. a sour substance _____
6. to fit to new circumstances _____
7. another name for antenna _____
8. the work of producing crops _____
9. landing place for aircraft _____
10. a warning or danger sign _____
11. sensitive to a specific substance _____
12. animal living on water and land _____
13. heavy object in water to prevent drifting _____
14. round, red fruit _____
15. the science of numbers _____
16. tube carrying blood _____
17. powder left after burning _____
18. science of the stars and planets _____

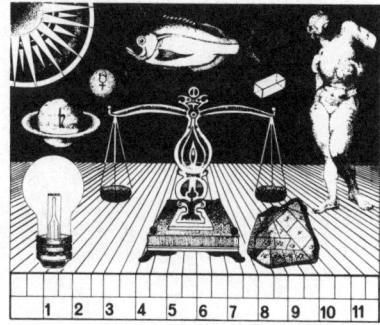

NAME	DATE
GRADE	TEACHER

THE SCIENCES

Each definition will give you a clue about a special kind of science. After reading the definition, unscramble the letters and spell out the correct science. A first letter clue will assist you.

1. y c o l o g e
   e _ _ _ _ _

   The science that deals with living things and their environment.

2. y o g l e o g
   g _ _ _ _ _ _

   The science that deals with the study of the earth and rocks.

3. b o g l o i y
   b _ _ _ _ _

   The study of life.

4. y o t a n b
   b _ _ _ _ _

   The science dealing with the study of plants.

5. c h i s s y p
   p _ _ _ _ _ _

   The science that studies natural laws and properties.

6. d e n i m i e c
   m _ _ _ _ _ _ _

   The science that studies the illnesses and diseases of the body.

7. s c h o o l y p y g
   p s y _ _ _ _ _ _

   The science dealing with animal and human behavior.

8. g o o l o y z   The science that studies
   z _ _ _ _ _ _   animals and the animal king-
        dom.

9. g o l o i c o s y   The science of human re-
   s _ _ _ _ _ _ _ _   lations.

10. t r o a s n o m y   The science that studies outer
    a _ _ _ _ _ _ _ _   space.

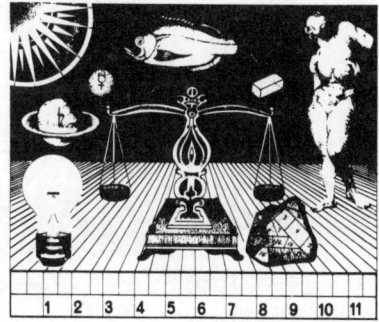

FINDING SCIENCE WORDS WITH "B"

Each of these science terms begins with the letter B. Read each statement and then write the correct word.

1. opposite of front _____
2. spherical object used in sports _____
3. large, airtight bag with gas that rises _____
4. land along a river _____
5. outside covering of a tree _____
6. glass container with flat ends _____
7. a type of fish _____
8. to set on fire _____
9. a small insect _____
10. a small stream _____
11. a flower grows from this _____
12. liquid part that flows through heart _____
13. used with an arrow _____
14. gives us our body shape _____
15. a color of the sky _____
16. smooth surface to write on in school _____
17. to seize with the teeth _____
18. the cutting part of a knife _____

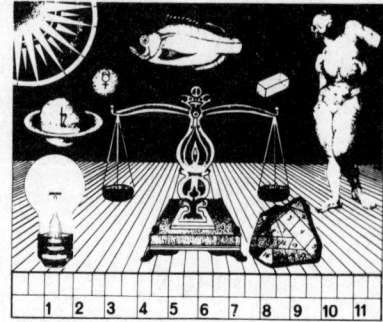

DOUBLE LETTER SCIENCE WORDS

Each of the words printed below has a double letter. Read the definition and then write the correct science word next to it.

1. ___b b___   small furry animal with long ears
2. ___c c_____   furry animal with a masked face and ringed tail
3. ___d d___   holds rider on a horse
4. ___e e___   when liquid becomes a solid
5. ___f f_____   to kill by cutting off air
6. ___g g___   a flock of geese
7. ____k k_____   a small cutting tool
8. ___o o__   red fluid in the body
9. _ll_____   a large reptile found in warm climates
10. _m m_____ bullets, bombs, rockets, grenades
11. ___n n___   a large gun
12. _p p_____   a household machine
13. ___r r___   brightly colored bird with hooked beak
14. ___s s   plant that grows on rocks
15. ___t t____   stores electricity
16. _____u u_   absence of air
17. ___z z___   found at the end of a hose

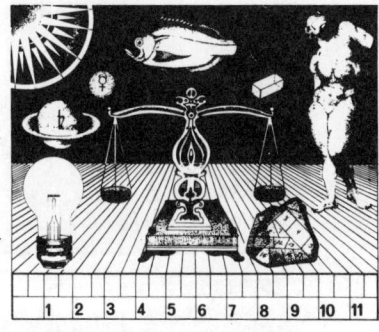

When you connect the dots, you will find a popular type of plant.

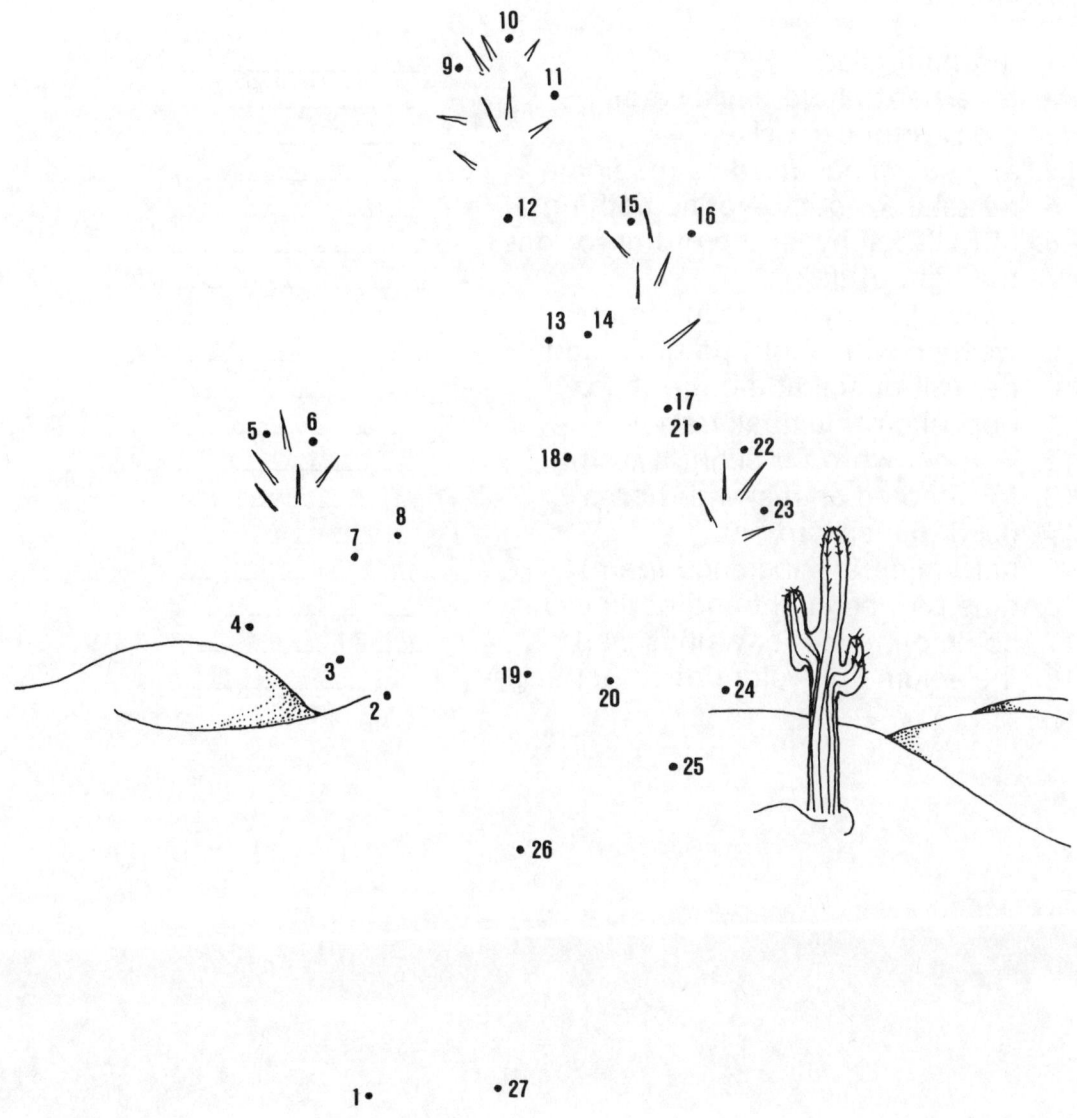

10
9•   •
    •11

•12   15•   •16

13• •14

•17
21•
18•   •22

5• •6   •23

7•   •8

4•
3•
19•   20•   •24   2•

•25

•26

1•   •27

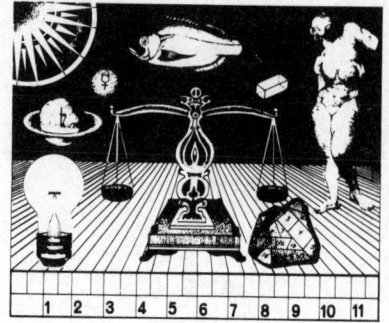

FINDING SCIENCE WORDS WITH "D"

Each of the science definitions below describes a word beginning with the letter D.

1. morning mist _____
2. a barrier to hold back water _____
3. a powerful explosive _____
4. any substance used as medicine _____
5. a sketch or outline of something _____
6. to collapse by letting out air or gas _____
7. the light of day _____
8. a type of playful ocean mammal _____
9. weapon with short, pointed blade _____
10. deposit of soil at mouth of sea _____
11. opposite of number 7 above _____
12. weather word for slight moisture _____
13. four-footed animal with horns _____
14. used to measure heat _____
15. hard mineral substance (gem) _____
16. time between light and darkness _____
17. common name for a physician _____
18. the volume of weight of something _____

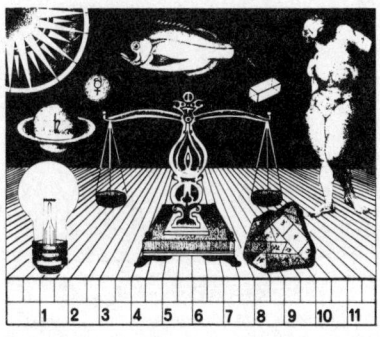

MATCHING SCIENCE TERMS

Read each of the following statements. Select the correct answer from the list at the bottom and write it next to the statement.

1. an untested idea in science _____
2. a natural satellite _____
3. the wearing away of land by water _____
4. the galaxy in which we live _____
5. the remains of plants and animals _____
6. approximate age of the earth _____
7. smallest unit of an element in science _____
8. rapid movement of masses of rock _____
9. units in which long periods of time are grouped _____
10. name of our present science age _____
11. large moving blocks of ice _____
12. transportation in space _____

fossil	eras
iceberg	metamorphic
space shuttle	atom
computer age	Milky Way
hypothesis	moon
avalanche	igneous
5 billion years	erosion
radioactivity	nuclear age

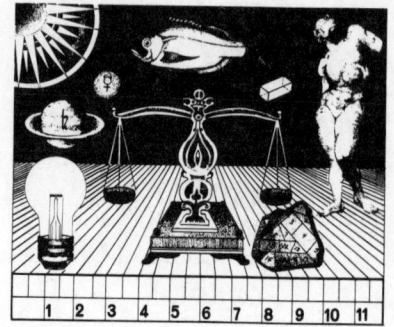

FINDING SCIENCE WORDS WITH "H"

Each of the science words below starts with the letter H. After reading the definition, write the correct word in the space provided.

1. area or place where an animal lives _____
2. a bright ring around the moon or sun _____
3. four-footed animal used for riding _____
4. a small rodent used as a pet and in experiments _____
5. a bird of prey _____
6. a group of animals together _____
7. something we all need to keep in the best of condition _____
8. muscular organ that pumps blood _____
9. a type of aircraft with spinning blades _____
10. a type of gas used in dirigibles or blimps _____
11. a female chicken _____
12. to sleep in the wintertime _____
13. a type of tree _____
14. foot of a horse and other animals _____
15. passed down from father to son _____
16. a male deer _____
17. a short, small-handled ax _____

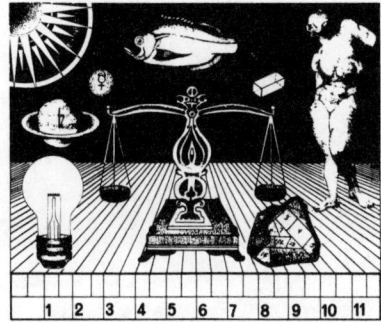

FIND THE WRONG WORD

In each group of five words below, there is one word that does not really belong with the group. Circle the word that you think does *not* belong there. Then, on the line below, state the reason why you have selected that particular word.

1. hand/toe/nose/lung/arm

_____

2. comet/meteor/asteroid/satellite/orbit

_____

3. lever/pulley/inclined plane/generator/wedge

_____

4. air/ice/water/gas/solid

_____

5. motorcycle/truck/tricycle/bicycle/unicycle

_____

6. bicycle/truck/automobile/roller skate/skateboard

_____

7. telephone/telegraph/television/typewriter/tree

_____

8. marble/iron/granite/quartz/brick

_____

9. typewriter/pen/chalk/pencil/crayon

_____

10. saw/nail/wrench/carpenter/ruler

_____

11. whale/porpoise/walrus/turtle/leopard

_____

12. chair/sofa/table/bench/hassock

_____

How did you do? Here are some harder ones!

13. battery/iron/electricity/lightning/candle

_____

14. gasoline/wood/alcohol/kerosene/oil

_____

15. vulture/duck/turkey/chicken/pheasant

_____

16. insect/reptile/lion/mammal/fish

_____

17. book/magazine/newspaper/road map/record

_____

18. wool/nylon/cotton/linen/silk

_____

19. steps/door/window/floor/wall

_____

20. century/month/decade/day/time

_____

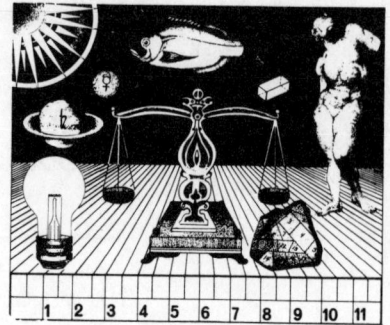

FINDING SCIENCE WORDS WITH "L"

Read each statement and then write the correct word beginning with the letter L which answers it.

1. a form of energy that lets us see _____
2. another word for work _____
3. a baby sheep _____
4. distance north and south of equator _____
5. melted rock from a volcano _____
6. part of the eyelid _____
7. member of the cat family with spots _____
8. to raise up like a winch does _____
9. flash of light in the sky _____
10. a fluid _____
11. having life _____
12. a large part of a tree _____
13. wood cut into boards _____
14. distance east and west _____
15. not firmly fastened _____
16. king of the beasts _____
17. tower with a light to guide ships _____
18. a long rope with a noose at the end _____

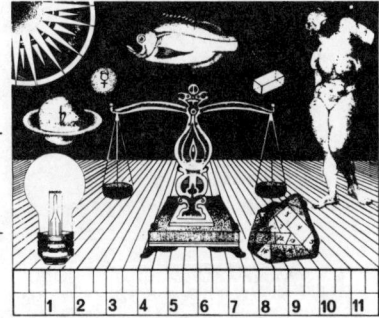

Connect these dots and find a living thing.

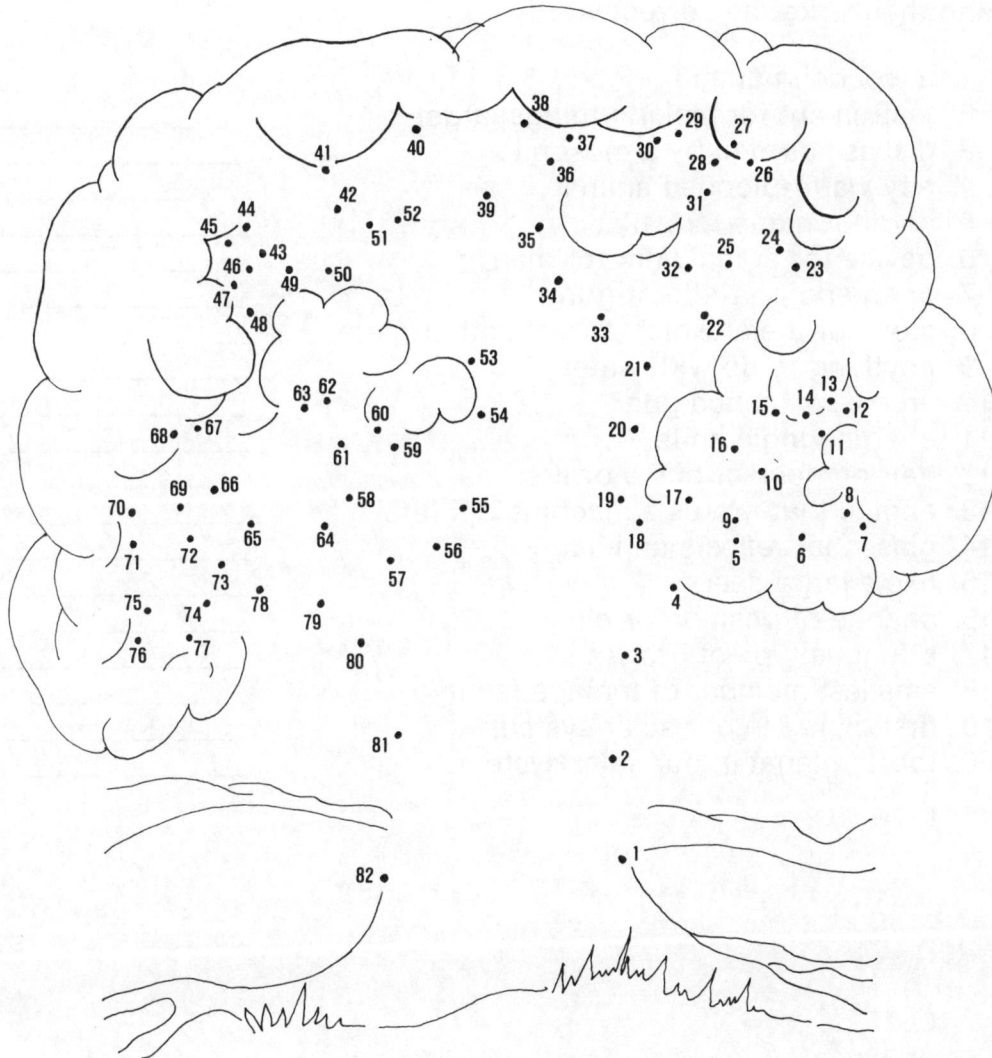

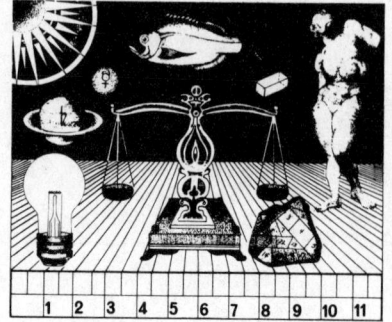

FINDING SCIENCE WORDS WITH "M"

Here are some science words that begin with M. Look at the definition and then write the correct word.

1. a wooden hammer _____
2. instrument for making things larger _____
3. disease carried by a mosquito _____
4. any warm-blooded animal _____
5. another name for sailor _____
6. device for doing work for man _____
7. open end of a rifle or gun _____
8. stone or metal which attracts other metal _____
9. anything to do with water _____
10. an old-fashioned gun _____
11. a large jungle knife _____
12. hair on neck of horse or lion _____
13. engine that makes a machine operate _____
14. glass that reflects an image _____
15. like a large deer _____
16. change of position or place _____
17. a fungus type of growth _____
18. smallest member of the ape family _____
19. first planet in our solar system _____
20. fourth planet in our solar system _____

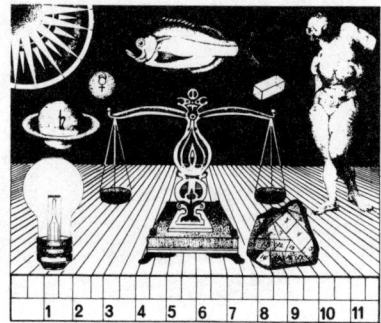

NAME _____ DATE _____

GRADE _____ TEACHER _____

A MOTOR

A motor is a machine that takes electrical energy and converts it into mechanical energy. There are many appliances and machines in your home that use motors. List at least ten of these motor-powered machines. (Example: a washing machine)

1. _____ 6. _____
2. _____ 7. _____
3. _____ 8. _____
4. _____ 9. _____
5. _____ 10. _____

Motors come in different sizes. The unit of measure used in a motor is called a unit of *horsepower*. Therefore, a 5-horsepower motor would do the same amount of work as five horses. A 1½-horsepower motor would do the same amount of work as 1½ horses. Can you locate the plates on the motors in your house and determine the horsepower of each motor? To be safe, make sure to unplug the cord from the outlet first.

Which do you think would use more electricity and have a bigger motor? Place a check next to the correct item:

1. _____a hair dryer or_____a radio?
2. _____an iron or_____a toaster?
3. _____a television set or_____a power saw?
4. _____a clothes dryer or_____an oven?
5. _____an electric clock or_____a can opener?

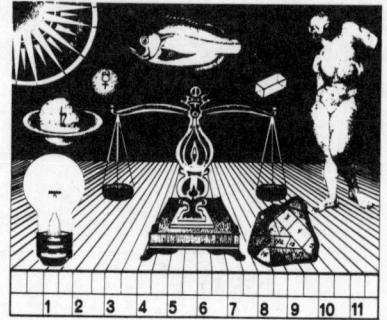

ANIMAL SOUNDS

Almost all animals make some sounds. Fill in the name of the animal you think makes the particular sound listed below.

1. caw _____
2. hiss _____
3. oink _____
4. neigh _____
5. yelp _____
6. roar _____
7. quack _____
8. trumpet _____
9. tweet _____
10. howl _____
11. hoot _____
12. bleat _____
13. buzz _____
14. gobble _____
15. croak _____
16. meow _____
17. snort _____
18. purr _____
19. squeak _____
20. growl _____

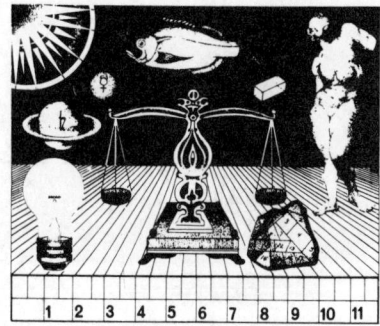

FINDING SCIENCE WORDS WITH "P"

The words described below are all science words that begin with the letter P. Read the definitions and then fill in the words which you think match them.

1. a step (as in walking) _____
2. wooden instrument used for rowing _____
3. a liquid used to protect wood and metal _____
4. the inner surface of your hand _____
5. a small tablet used in medicine _____
6. an image recorded by a camera _____
7. a person licensed to operate aircraft _____
8. a type of evergreen tree _____
9. a hollow tube to carry water, gas, or other fluids _____
10. part of a motor in a car _____
11. clear fluid part of the blood used in transfusions _____
12. a substance which causes injury or death if swallowed _____
13. a small body of water _____
14. an ocean mammal that breathes air _____
15. a mark or impression on wood, paper, or metal _____
16. a throbbing felt in your wrist _____
17. a long snake that coils and crushes its prey _____

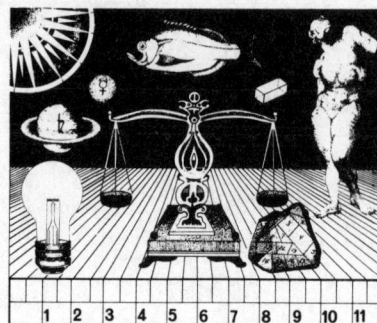

MORE WORD SCRAMBLES

Unscramble each of these sets of letters to form the name of a type of fruit:

1. slump   _____
2. shericre   _____
3. scheape   _____
4. lapsep   _____
5. saperg   _____
6. sangero   _____
7. sananba   _____
8. lineapepp   _____
9. spear   _____
10. tropsica   _____

Unscramble these names of nuts:

1. teapnu   _____
2. domnal   _____
3. lazeh   _____
4. lizabr   _____
5. washec   _____
6. lawutn   _____
7. napec   _____
8. stapchioi   _____

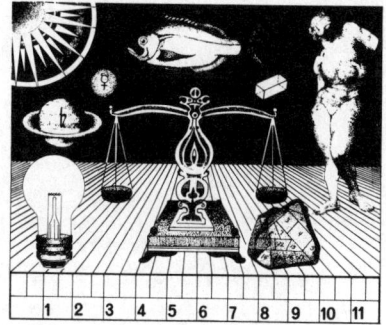

WEAPONS OF WAR

Can you find all of the weapons listed below in this puzzle?

```
T G D M O R T A R B A Y S
A A A U A S S F L I N T E
N T G S P A W Z Z U B C R
K L G K B G W O L B A U O
S I E E O R S O R E Y T C
H N R T N A D R W D O L K
W G M A C E A O O A N A E
O N I M P T B E N N E S T
R E W R S K N I F E T S A
R L O T S I P B E R W S O
A T E N O N N A C G T O W
```

arrow	cutlass	mace	saber
bayonet	dagger	mortar	sword
blow (gun)	flint	musket	tank
bow	gatling	pistol	tear gas
buzz (bomb)	grenade	rocket	torpedo
cannon	knife		

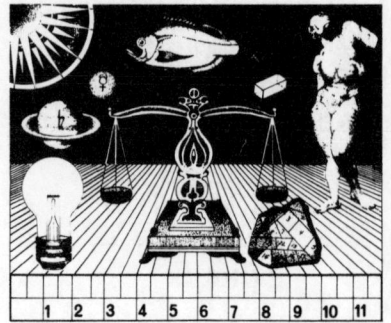

ANIMAL USES

Here are the names of some familiar animals. List one way in which people use each animal:

1. reindeer _____
2. chimpanzee _____
3. alligator _____
4. water buffalo _____
5. camel _____
6. cat _____
7. sheep _____
8. snake _____
9. elephant _____
10. mule _____
11. leopard _____
12. donkey _____
13. cow _____
14. goat _____
15. rabbit _____
16. llama _____
17. kangaroo _____
18. panda _____
19. seal _____
20. skunk _____

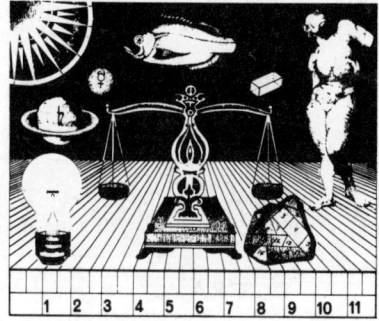

FINDING SCIENCE WORDS WITH "R"

Here are the definitions of some interesting science words, all beginning with the letter R. Read each clue and write the correct word next to it.

1. long-eared and soft-fur mammal _____
2. transmits sounds you listen to _____
3. floating structure of logs and boards _____
4. a road with parallel steel bars _____
5. a sloping walk, simple machine _____
6. a harsh voice sound _____
7. a beam of light _____
8. to take down for future use _____
9. to throw back light _____
10. a large deer found in the northern regions _____
11. place where water is stored _____
12. to go backwards in motion _____
13. grains of food grown in water _____
14. a large mass of stone _____
15. device driven by gases escaping from the rear of it _____
16. to go around _____
17. a clear, deep red gem _____
18. reddish brown coating formed on iron or steel by moisture _____

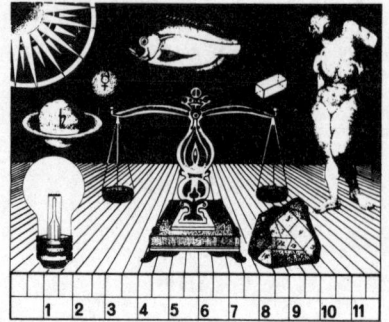

TYPES OF SCIENTISTS

Scientists have become specialized in their areas of study and have specific titles. Match each of these job descriptions with the correct title from the list at the bottom of the page.

_____ 1. Person who studies water
_____ 2. Person who studies the rocks and their formations
_____ 3. Person who studies the heavens
_____ 4. Person who studies plants
_____ 5. Person who studies physical laws and properties
_____ 6. Person who studies ancient ruins
_____ 7. Person who studies the environment and conservation
_____ 8. Person who studies the mixing and properties of chemicals
_____ 9. Person who studies animal life
_____ 10. Person who studies living organisms
_____ 11. Person who studies the weather
_____ 12. Person who studies reptiles

A. Chemist   G. Meteorologist
B. Herpetologist   H. Geologist
C. Physicist   I. Astronomer
D. Biologist   J. Zoologist
E. Ecologist   K. Hydrologist
F. Archeologist   L. Botanist

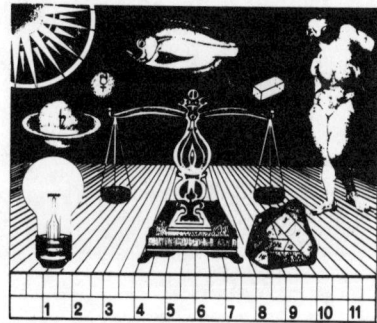

FINDING SCIENCE WORDS WITH "S"

The science words defined below all begin with S. Read each definition and then write the correct word next to it.

1. freedom from danger   _____
2. moisture in the mouth   _____
3. a type of fish which jumps upstream   _____
4. closest star to the earth   _____
5. small, gritty particles of rock   _____
6. planet with rings around it   _____
7. tool for cutting wood   _____
8. small particles on side of a fish   _____
9. an animal that feeds on dead animals   _____
10. a body of knowledge about natural things in the
    universe   _____
11. tool for cutting paper   _____
12. used to weigh things   _____
13. a metal pin with threads on it   _____
14. covering of skin on your head   _____
15. a large body of water   _____
16. deposit at bottom of river or lake   _____
17. large scissors   _____
18. hard outer casing of some sea life   _____

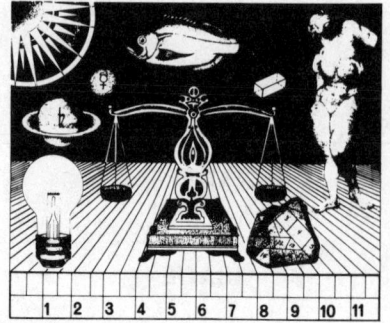

SCRAMBLED SCIENCE OBJECTS

Rearrange each of these scrambled words to spell the name of an object (animal or thing) that has to do with science. Sometimes the letters will spell more than one word, but write down only the science word.

1. sale _____
2. ample _____
3. rats _____
4. sleet _____
5. ramble _____
6. lamp _____
7. heart _____
8. risen _____
9. emit _____
10. eat _____
11. prides _____
12. paws _____
13. cheap _____
14. seaside _____
15. flow _____
16. shore _____
17. flier _____
18. mean _____

Combined Activities

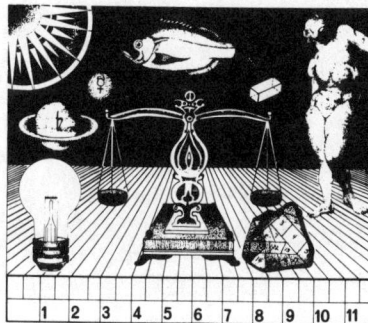

WORDS WITHIN WORDS

In each of the words below you will find a smaller word related to science. Read the clue on the right and then fill in the word.

1. warming   _____   part of the body
2. gardens   _____   home for animals
3. jowls   _____   bird of prey
4. pinches   _____   unit of measurement
5. iceboat   _____   a snake
6. candles   _____   a container
7. crowds   _____   a bird
8. spearmint _____   a fruit
9. furniture _____   protective covering
10. meantime _____   small insect
11. kitchen   _____   bothers you
12. cloaks   _____   a tree
13. acorn   _____   a vegetable
14. suspense _____   writing instrument
15. licorice _____   grows in water
16. paper   _____   large mammal
17. keel   _____   a fish
18. knitwear _____   picks up vibrations

Combined Activities

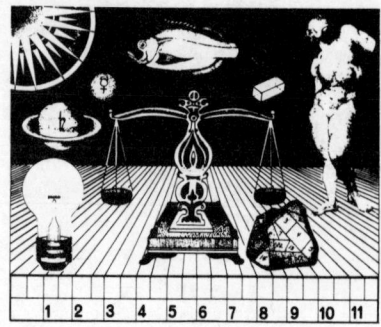

FINDING SCIENCE WORDS WITH "T"

Read each statement carefully. Fill in the correct science word beginning with the letter T.

1. rear part of an animal's body _____
2. change from a wild state to domestic state _____
3. a sense using the tongue _____
4. salty drop from the eye _____
5. instrument used for talking _____
6. instrument for making distant objects appear closer _____
7. machine that shows pictures _____
8. attach muscles to bones _____
9. an untested idea in science _____
10. measures temperature _____
11. another word for a thin string _____
12. to fasten together _____
13. measure of minutes and hours _____
14. a circle of rubber _____
15. an explosive used for blasting _____
16. part of a foot _____
17. three-wheeled cycle _____

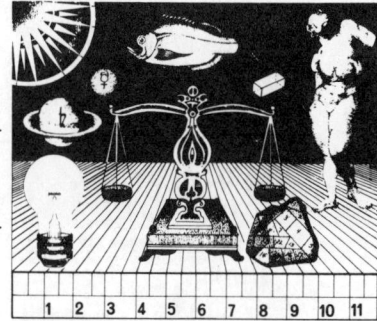

MATCHING TERM REVIEW

Match each term in Column B with the correct word in Column A.

	Column A	*Column B*
_____	1. liquid	mile
_____	2. orbit	Uranus
_____	3. exhaled gas	gas
_____	4. alligator	measured by degrees
_____	5. motion	mollusk
_____	6. basketball	0 degree freeze
_____	7. granite	inclined plane
_____	8. fuel	movement
_____	9. density	volume measure
_____	10. oxygen	path
_____	11. temperature	igneous rock
_____	12. measurement	sound waves
_____	13. planet	definite shape
_____	14. solid	H_2O
_____	15. simple machine	frog
_____	16. water	CO_2
_____	17. vibrations	sphere
_____	18. clam	reptile
_____	19. Celsius	water
_____	20. amphibian	gasoline

- -

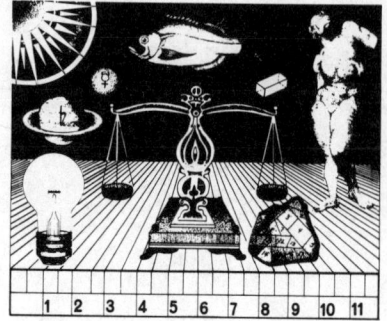

SCIENCE OPPOSITES

Write the *antonym*, or opposite word, for each of the science terms listed. Think carefully, because some of the answers may be tricky.

1. land _____
2. wet _____
3. ocean _____
4. potential energy _____
5. geology _____
6. mammal _____
7. sun _____
8. conservation _____
9. artificial _____
10. oil _____
11. dry _____
12. liquid _____
13. plain _____
14. valley _____
15. creek _____
16. copper _____
17. horsepower _____
18. noise _____
19. hand _____
20. wrist _____

Write a sentence containing each of the following words:

1. artificial

_____

2. horsepower

_____

3. plain

_____

4. geology

_____

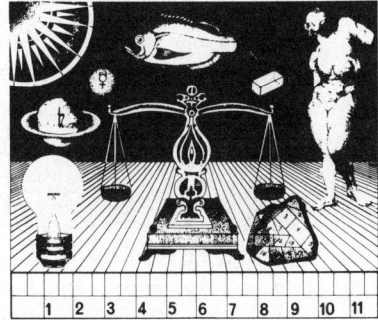

TRANSPORTATION CHECKUP

Here is a list of *transportation* vehicles. Write a short phrase or sentence about each one.

1. submarine

_____

2. glider

_____

3. escalator

_____

4. moped

_____

5. monorail

_____

6. canoe

_____

7. automobile

_____

8. blimp

_____

9. elevator

_____

10. subway

_____

11. helicopter

_____

12. rocket

_____

13. ferry

_____

14. snowmobile

_____

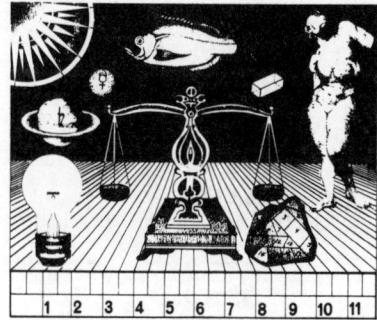

FINDING SCIENCE WORDS WITH "W"

All of the science terms answering the definitions below start with the letter W. Read each definition and then write the proper word next to it.

 1. largest ocean mammal   _____
 2. large body of moving air   _____
 3. large, doglike animal   _____
 4. a shrill, clear sound   _____
 5. used to make candles   _____
 6. long, slender, bendable metal   _____
 7. deep pit for storing water   _____
 8. hair from a sheep used to make clothing   _____
 9. how heavy something is   _____
10. machine for pulling or lifting   _____
11. simple tool used for splitting wood or metal   _____
12. joint that connects hand with arm   _____
13. direction of the sunset   _____
14. covered or soaked with water   _____
15. coldest of the four seasons   _____
16. when two nations fight   _____
17. circular object that turns   _____
18. conditions of the atmosphere that change daily   _____

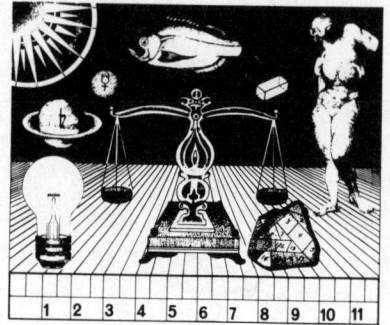

SPORTS WORDS

Many people like to watch sports and many people participate in sports. See how many different sports you can think of by answering the following questions:

1. List five sports that involve a *sphere* or ball.

   a. _____
   b. _____
   c. _____
   d. _____
   e. _____

2. List three sports that use *wheels*:

   a. _____
   b. _____
   c. _____

3. List five sports that involve snow or ice:

   a. _____
   b. _____
   c. _____
   d. _____
   e. _____

4. List six sports that involve *water*:

   a. _____   d. _____
   b. _____   e. _____
   c. _____   f. _____

5. List six sports that involve *air*:

   a. _____   d. _____
   b. _____   e. _____
   c. _____   f. _____

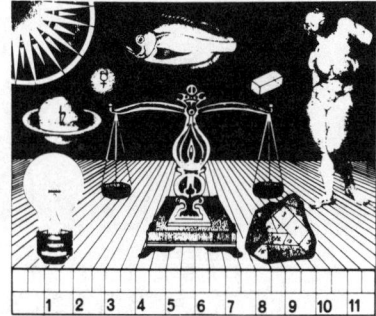

VEGETABLE PARTS

A vegetable is a living thing. It is a plant and it can be purchased fresh, canned, frozen, or dried. Fresh vegetables are called *produce*. Some vegetables are available all year round. These include potatoes, carrots, and celery. Other vegetables are seasonal and can only be bought in spring or summer. They include green beans, asparagus, and corn. Some vegetables are grown in the wintertime in southern warm states and are shipped north.

The *fruit* of a vegetable plant has a high water content and is low in calories. Such vegetable fruits include cucumber, eggplant, okra, pepper, and squash.

The *flower* of a vegetable plant also has a high water content and is low in calories. These flowers include cauliflower and broccoli.

The *stem* of a vegetable plant is also high in water content and low in calories. Stems that we eat are the asparagus and celery.

The *seeds* of a vegetable plant store food. They are high in starch and high in calories. Some seeds that we eat are corn, beans, and peas.

The *leaf* of a vegetable plant is high in water content and low in calories. Leaf plants that we eat are cabbage, collard greens, dandelion, lettuce, mustard greens, spinach, and Brussels sprouts.

Bulbs that we eat from plants include onions and garlic.

Roots of a plant that we eat are high in starch and high in calories. Some common roots include beets, carrots, radishes, rutabaga, and turnips.

A *tuber* of a plant stores food, like other roots and bulbs. A potato is an example of a tuber.

1. List eight different types of vegetables:

a. _____   e. _____
b. _____   f. _____
c. _____   g. _____
d. _____   h. _____

2. List two examples of stems that we eat.

    a. _____

    b. _____

3. List three examples of plant seeds:

    a. _____

    b. _____

    c. _____

4. Which parts of a plant are high in starch and high in calories?

_____

5. List some of the leaves that we eat from vegetables:

    a. _____

    b. _____

    c. _____

    d. _____

    e. _____

    f. _____

6. List four examples of plant fruit:

    a. _____

    b. _____

    c. _____

    d. _____

REVIEW EXERCISES

INTRODUCTION TO THE TEACHER

This section contains a series of checkup exercises for all of the body of knowledge contained in this book. They are not tests, but can be so employed as a form of evaluating children's accumulated knowledge and understanding of the information presented.

The science review questions are completion questions and depend on the students' ability to recall. The true-false questions allow them to recall and make inferences and comparisons. The science crossout section will test ability to relate information and classify it into proper categories. The alphabetization review will strengthen their basic ability to classify terms according to spelling rules.

Each of the evaluation exercises should help the students by having them review the incorrect answers on their worksheets. It is suggested that every child keep a folder of his or her papers. Constant review and basic reference will help the student master these questions.

9

SCIENCE REVIEW #1

The questions below will test your memory on some of the activities you have already done. See how many of these you can get correct.

1. All mammals that have backbones are called _____.
2. The tail of a fish acts like the _____ of a ship.
3. Elephant teeth and tusks are made of _____.
4. A shark, unlike other fish, does not have _____.
5. An animal that can live on land and in water is _____.
6. To be asleep in the wintertime is to _____.
7. Mollusks, unlike mammals, do not have _____.
8. The oyster produces a gem called the _____.
9. A favorite fish food of whales is the _____ in the water.
10. A bird of prey that hunts at night is the _____.
11. A fish breathes with its _____.
12. The blood is carried away from the heart by _____.
13. The moisture in your mouth is called _____.
14. An involuntary muscle is one that you _____ control.
15. A fast response to something is called _____.
16. The opening in your throat to the lungs is called the _____.
17. Purify is another word for _____.
18. The bone in your head that protects the brain is the _____.

SCIENCE REVIEW #2

Read each statement and answer it with the best possible answer. These are review questions and you should know the answer to each one.

1. A clam belongs to the _____ family.
2. The highest clouds in the sky are _____ clouds.
3. A mammal must breathe _____.
4. A whale is a _____ type of mammal.
5. Teeth that protrude from an elephant are called _____.
6. Predator is a word that means _____.
7. The outer ear acts as _____ in the hearing process.
8. Sea turtles are hunted for their _____.
9. A grasshopper is considered a _____ of the farmer.
10. The middle of a hurricane is called the _____.
11. A pump in the body is called the _____.
12. The liver produces a juice called _____ which aids in digestion.
13. A cough is considered the action of _____ (type) muscle.
14. The upper arm muscle is called the _____.
15. Fluid in the bone is called _____.
16. The pupil of the eye _____ with the amount of light.
17. Food in the body is mainly digested in the _____.
18. Wind speed is measured by an instrument called the _____.

SCIENCE REVIEW #3

Test your memory of what you have learned by reading each question below and filling in the space with the correct word.

1. A bone broken in more than one place is a _____ fracture.
2. The brain is divided into two parts called _____.
3. The nerve connecting the eye to the brain is called the _____ nerve.
4. The clear part of the eye that lets light through is called the _____.
5. The first 10 miles above the earth is called the _____.
6. Wind direction is shown by an instrument called the _____.
7. A form of speed measurement on water is called the _____.
8. All of the water in the world is called the _____ sphere.
9. Weather that is sticky and damp is called _____ weather.
10. The speed of wind is called _____.
11. The only known planet with rings around it is _____.
12. The study of outer space is called _____.
13. A unit of measurement in the solar system is the _____ year.
14. A large mass of rock/metal hurtling to earth from space is _____.
15. An instrument that measures walking distance is the _____.
16. A measure of energy in food is called the _____.
17. The measure of heat and cold is called _____.
18. The study of the earth's formation is called _____.

SCIENCE REVIEW #4

Can you answer all of these review questions? Read each one and then write the correct answer in the space provided.

1. The protection and care of natural resources is called _____.
2. The ability to do work is called _____.
3. A machine depends on some type of _____ to operate.
4. Movement is always present in _____ energy.
5. Mechanical energy comes from _____.
6. The natural home of an animal is its _____.
7. The wearing away of dirt and water is called _____.
8. Flying a kite would be an example of _____ power.
9. A sanitary landfill is also known as a _____.
10. Candle light is a form of _____ light.
11. The absence of air is called a _____.
12. Sounds that humans cannot hear are called _____ sounds.
13. An engine that does work is called a _____.
14. Matter without a definite size is called _____.
15. The human body exhales a poisonous gas called _____.
16. A lever is a form of _____.
17. Matter takes up space and has _____.
18. A dull, steady pain in the body is called _____.

REVIEW TRUE-FALSE QUESTIONS #1

Read each statement and then circle either T for True, or F for False.

T	F	1. Water mammals, like the porpoise, are not warm-blooded.
T	F	2. An elephant's nose is called a trunk.
T	F	3. Animals that are disappearing from the earth are called endangered species.
T	F	4. A shark has scales like other fish.
T	F	5. A bladder in a fish allows it to rise and sink.
T	F	6. The largest shark in the ocean is called a blue shark.
T	F	7. The crocodile and the shark are the same thing.
T	F	8. A water moccasin is also called a cotton mouth.
T	F	9. Reptiles belong to the vertebrate family.
T	F	10. A turtle does not hibernate.
T	F	11. A mollusk has a soft backbone.
T	F	12. Oysters are considered a seafood delicacy.
T	F	13. Black pearls are as common as white pearls.
T	F	14. A snake is considered a friend of the farmer.
T	F	15. An otter would be considered an amphibian.
T	F	16. Blood absorbs oxygen from the air we breathe.
T	F	17. A capillary is not considered a blood vessel.
T	F	18. There are five types of blood vessels.

- -

REVIEW TRUE-FALSE QUESTIONS #2

After you read each statement, circle whether it is True or False.

T   F   1. The heart beats 30 times per minute.

T   F   2. The stomach is part of the circulatory system.

T   F   3. There are three parts to the digestive system.

T   F   4. Saliva helps to break down food as it enters the mouth.

T   F   5. An enzyme is an internal organ in the stomach.

T   F   6. There are 300 muscles in the body.

T   F   7. A muscle connects two bones.

T   F   8. A voluntary muscle is one that you can control.

T   F   9. A ligament is a type of muscle.

T   F   10. The heart is the largest muscle in the body.

T   F   11. The expansion and contraction of the heart is called a heartbeat.

T   F   12. A tendon connects a muscle to a bone.

T   F   13. Nerves that are related to the senses are called *motor nerves*.

T   F   14. The word *motor* means movement or motion.

T   F   15. A reflex is a quick response to something.

T   F   16. The brain is the center of all nerves.

T   F   17. Lungs contain large air sacs.

T   F   18. Broken blood vessels in the nose can cause nosebleeds.

REVIEW TRUE-FALSE QUESTIONS #3

Check whether each statement is True or False.

T	F	1. An infection of the lungs is called tuberculosis.
T	F	2. Exhale refers to the air we breathe out.
T	F	3. Purify means to clean and improve something.
T	F	4. A broken bone heals from the outside in.
T	F	5. Food inside the bone is called *marrow*.
T	F	6. A broken bone is called a *fracture*.
T	F	7. The spinal cord is protected by the spinal column.
T	F	8. Nerves are found only in certain parts of the body.
T	F	9. The cranium is the protection cavity of the heart.
T	F	10. A cartilage is a type of muscle.
T	F	11. There are 60 bones in the body.
T	F	12. There are six senses in our body system.
T	F	13. Eyelashes have no useful purpose.
T	F	14. Tears in the eye help to wash out small particles.
T	F	15. A rupture of the eardrum can cause deafness.
T	F	16. Sound waves hitting the ear are called *vibrations*.
T	F	17. The word *transmit* means to hold something.
T	F	18. The tongue contains six different types of nerve cells.

- -

REVIEW TRUE-FALSE QUESTIONS #4

See if you can circle each answer correctly.

T	F	1. The taste bud is located in the throat.
T	F	2. The senses of smell and taste work together.
T	F	3. The tip of the tongue tastes salty things.
T	F	4. A cut in the skin is called a *bruise*.
T	F	5. Clogged pores in the skin can cause an infection.
T	F	6. The skin is not considered a sense organ.
T	F	7. The inner layer of the skin is called the *epidermis*.
T	F	8. A blow to the skin is called a *bruise*.
T	F	9. The word *offensive* means something you dislike.
T	F	10. The medical term for fingers is *phalanges*.
T	F	11. An illness in the body is called a *disease*.
T	F	12. The exosphere is the layer of air farthest from the earth's surface.
T	F	13. A meteorite is a burning body falling through space.
T	F	14. Satellites help scientists to predict the weather.
T	F	15. The speed of wind is called *velocity*.
T	F	16. A knot is not a unit of measurement.
T	F	17. A cloud contains water vapor which later can become rain.
T	F	18. A tornado and a hurricane are the same.

SCIENCE CROSSOUT #1

In each group of four words listed, there is one word that does not fit in with the rest. Cross out the word that you think does not fit.

1.	ecology	geology	astronomy	biology
2.	clam	turtle	oyster	lobster
3.	wind	water	motor	solar
4.	radius	humerus	ulna	ankle
5.	tornado	hurricane	typhoon	ocean
6.	marrow	artery	capillary	vein
7.	muscle	tendon	ligament	bone
8.	teeth	skull	ribs	epidermis
9.	trout	catfish	tuna	eel
10.	lung	gill	fin	scales
11.	pearl	ruby	diamond	emerald
12.	boa	python	copperhead	garter snake
13.	sand	granite	rock	meteor
14.	shark	snake	alligator	turtle
15.	hide	skin	hair	fur

Review Exercises

SCIENCE CROSSOUT #2

Cross out the word in each group that does not relate to the other three.

1. three	plant	roots	flower
2. fog	smog	mist	duststorm
3. truck	bicycle	automobile	tractor
4. sewing	stove	dryer	pressing iron
5. solid	liquid	gas	evaporation
6. purify	contaminate	clean	sterile
7. wood	cork	paper	copper
8. hammer	bench	drill	saw
9. orbit	reflection	light	refraction
10. blue	rainbow	violet	heat
11. magma	volcano	limestone	lava
12. steamship	canoe	boat	kayak
13. wave	tide	force	typhoon
14. horse	colt	mare	hybrid
15. balloon	box	bottle	can
16. smell	touch	digest	hear

ALPHABETIZATION REVIEW #1

Alphabetize these words. Be careful of your answers. Use numbers 1–20.

1. _____ scientist
2. _____ botanist
3. _____ energy
4. _____ mammal
5. _____ planet
6. _____ environment
7. _____ orbit
8. _____ biology
9. _____ horse
10. _____ machine
11. _____ solar
12. _____ motor
13. _____ ecology
14. _____ conservation
15. _____ helium
16. _____ shark
17. _____ muscle
18. _____ heart
19. _____ blood
20. _____ pressure

ALPHABETIZATION REVIEW #2

Alphabetize these science terms in correct order by using numbers 1-20. Think carefully as you do this exercise.

1. _____ reflex
2. _____ purify
3. _____ thunder
4. _____ reflection
5. _____ lightning
6. _____ refraction
7. _____ tornado
8. _____ cyclone
9. _____ tusk
10. _____ hurricane
11. _____ snake
12. _____ pupil
13. _____ elephant
14. _____ velocity
15. _____ thermometer
16. _____ weather
17. _____ tibia
18. _____ measurement
19. _____ circulation
20. _____ knot

- -

ALPHABETIZATION REVIEW #3

These science terms should be alphabetized correctly by using the numbers 1-20. This exercise is a little more difficult.

1. _____ pace
2. _____ paint
3. _____ puddle
4. _____ pilot
5. _____ pine
6. _____ pulse
7. _____ printing
8. _____ python
9. _____ pipe
10. _____ photographer
11. _____ palm
12. _____ photo
13. _____ pill
14. _____ plane
15. _____ poison
16. _____ plasma
17. _____ porpoise
18. _____ penguin
19. _____ paddle
20. _____ person

ALPHABETIZATION REVIEW #4

Look at each word carefully and place it in its proper alphabetical order. Use numbers 1-20 in this activity.

1. _____ fuel
2. _____ fire
3. _____ fin
4. _____ finger
5. _____ flashing
6. _____ ache
7. _____ ash
8. _____ appliance
9. _____ astronomy
10. _____ animal
11. _____ conservation
12. _____ cranium
13. _____ crow
14. _____ creature
15. _____ chemical
16. _____ winch
17. _____ wind
18. _____ waterfall
19. _____ vein
20. _____ winter

ANSWER KEY

NOTE TO THE TEACHER

In some of these exercises the students' answers may vary. Therefore, for those exercises in which a variety of answers may appear, the symbol AWV (answers will vary) will appear in the answer key.

No answers have been listed for the reading comprehension exercises, as the students' phraseology may vary considerably in answering these questions.

All other answers have been provided for you. Remember, more than one correct answer may be possible.

page 18	whale	page 29	AWV

page 18	whale
page 19	1. deer
	2. horse
	3. elephant
	4. skunk
	5. cattle
	6. porcupine
	7. sheep
	8. donkey
	9. owl
	10. fox
	11. eagle
	12. snake
	13. swine
	14. lion
	15. otter
	16. kangaroo
page 22	1. ro
	2. peli
	3. her/falc
	4. h
	5. cr
	6. spar
	7. chic
	8. swal
	9. nightin
	10. qu
	11. th
	12. os
	13. sand
	14. f
	15. part
page 26	1. e
	2. d
	3. c
	4. j
	5. k
	6. g
	7. h
	8. a
	9. b
	10. i
	11. f
	12. l

page 29	AWV
page 32	starfish
page 37	1. seal
	2. mane
	3. maple
	4. tablet
	5. peach
	6. lead
	7. tide
	8. wasp
	9. earth
	10. rifle
	11. wolf
	12. horse
	13. lair
	14. lemon
	15. owl
	16. steel
	17. plane
	18. thorn
page 40	turtle
page 41	AWV
page 42	1. walrus
	2. oceans
	3. vibrations
	4. clams
	5. leopard
	6. reptile
	7. pearls
	Circled word is *animals*.
page 43	AWV
page 44	See Word Fun answer key
page 45	1. shark
	2. mollusk
	3. rudder
	4. turtle
	5. fins
	6. hibernate
	7. mammals
	8. plankton
	9. predator
	10. sparrow

	11. elephant
	12. owl
	13. gills
	14. oyster
	15. reptile
	16. leopard
	17. amphibian
	18. scales
page 49	heart
page 50	1. pupil
	2. temple
	3. palm
	4. calf
	5. trunk
	6. nail
	7. tongue
	8. arms
	9. eye
	10. teeth
	11. nose
	12. hair
	13. drum
	14. lash
page 53	1. bones
	2. eyes
	3. arm
	4. elbow/bowel
	5. brain
	6. mouth
	7. vein
	8. heart
	9. toes
	10. ears
	11. nose
	12. teeth
	13. wrist
	14. tonsil
	15. chest
page 58	AWV
page 63	8, 1, 3, 10, 11,
	12, 9, 6, 7, 5, 2, 4, 13
page 66	See Word Fun answer key
page 77	1. heart
	2. stomach
	3. bones
	4. lungs
	5. nose
	6. eye
	7. tongue
	8. skin
	9. brain
	10. neck
	11. fingers
	12. mouth
page 80	1. bones
	2. nerves
	3. mouth

	4. narcotics
	5. senses
	6. tongue
	Circled word is *bruise*.
page 81	AWV
page 82	See Word Fun answer key
page 83	1. pupil
	2. cells
	3. iris
	4. tongue
	5. motor
	6. contract
	7. fracture
	8. saliva
	9. bicep
	10. marrow
	11. rupture
	12. infection
	13. cartilage
	14. capillary
	15. stomach
	16. muscle
page 101	AWV
page 102	1. knots
	2. thunder
	3. flood
	4. meteor
	5. humid
	6. snowy
	Circled word is *stormy*.
page 103	AWV
page 104	See Word Fun answer key
page 105	1. direction
	2. hydrosphere
	3. weather
	4. energy
	5. hurricane
	6. flood
	7. wind
	8. atmosphere
	9. ocean
	10. evaporation
	11. knot
	12. tornado
	13. meteor
	14. humid
	15. velocity
page 111	1. start
	2. custom
	3. plumber
	4. raisin
	The planet is *Saturn*.
page 112	AWV
page 115	1. July 1969
	2. Pacific Ocean
	3. Neil Armstrong

4. three
5. doctors, designers, engineers etc.
6. President John F. Kennedy

page 116 See Word Fun answer key

page 119
1. hydrosphere
2. biosphere
3. lithosphere
4. troposphere
5. atmosphere
6. hemisphere
7. stratosphere
8. exosphere
9. ionosphere

page 120
1. moon
2. Mercury
3. sun
4. Saturn
5. Mercury
6. Jupiter
7. comet
8. Earth
9. meteor
10. Mars
11. eclipse
12. Mars
13. stars
14. galaxy

page 121 AWV

page 122
1. star
2. planets
3. comet
4. orbit
5. moon
6. rotation
7. rocket
8. Mars
9. sunny
Circled word is *astronomy*.

page 123 AWV

page 124 See Word Fun answer key

page 125
1. planets
2. revolution
3. universe
4. earth
5. orbit
6. rotation
7. telescope
8. year
9. astronomy
10. Mars
11. Venus
12. space
13. astronomer
14. moon

15. sun
16. galaxy
17. astronaut

page 129
1. 85
2. 60
3. 5
4. 35
5. 10
6. 30
7. 21
8. 15
9. 0
10. 90

page 130 AWV

page 132 220, 405, 335, 740

page 134
1. 25.40
2. 157.48
3. 11
4. ¼
5. 4.8
6. 13.3
7. 10
8. 250
9. 255.905
10. 20
11. 30.48

page 136
1. Indian
2. Pacific
3. Africa and Asia
4. 130 million square miles
5. North America
6. 52¼ million square miles
7. 2½
8. Arctic
9. Indian
10. North America
11. Pacific/Atlantic
12. Australia

page 138
1. 5:00 p.m.
2. 9-12
3. 11-6, 1-5, 3-4
4. 9-6, 11-5, 1-4, 2-3
5. 8-9, 12-1:00
6. 12°, 14°, 10°
7. 16
8. 10
9. 3-4, 2-3
10. 6, 6

page 140
1. d
2. i
3. e
4. h
5. b
6. l
7. j
8. c
9. g

	10. f		a. machines
	11. a		b. the sun
	12. k		c. a flow of electrons
page 141	1. g		d. storage battery
	2. h		e. fast moving molecules
	3. k		f. splitting atoms
	4. p	**page 154**	AWV
	5. a	**page 155**	AWV
	6. o	**page 156**	1. f
	7. d		2. n
	8. j		3. e
	9. i		4. a
	10. b		5. h
	11. e		6. i
	12. l	**page 157**	1. h
	13. f		2. g
	14. m		3. l
	15. n		4. b
	16. c		5. f
page 142	1. measure		6. j
	2. degree		7. c
	3. time		8. i
	4. area		9. d
	5. calorie		10. k
	Circled word is *meter*.		11. e
			12. a
page 143	AWV	**page 158**	(top) AWV
page 144	See Word Fun answer key		(bottom) 1. n
			2. n
page 145	1. measure		3. n
	2. temperature		4. a
	3. calorie		5. n
	4. Arctic		6. a
	5. barometer		7. a
	6. continent		8. n
	7. pedometer		9. n
	8. Australia		10. n
	9. pressure	**page 159**	AWV
	10. Fahrenheit	**page 160**	1. inclined plane
	11. Europe		2. wheel/axle
	12. area		3. pulley
	13. meter		4. lever
	14. island		5. wheel/axle
	15. Celsius		6. lever
			7. inclined plane
page 149	AWV		8. wedge
page 150	a horseshoe magnet		9. lever
page 151	AWV		10. wheel/axle
page 152	AWV		11. wedge
page 153	a. p		12. pulley
	b. p		13. screw
	c. k		14. pulley
	d. p		15. wheel/axle
	e. p	**page 163**	AWV
	f. p	**page 164**	See Word Fun answer key
	g. k	**page 165**	AWV
	h. k		

page 168
1. 20
2. 110
3. 90
4. 60
5. 60
6. 100
7. 40
8. 130
9. 80
10. 20
11. 70
12. 40

page 170
1. machine
2. source
3. plants
4. fossils
5. power

Circled word is *motor*.

page 171   AWV

page 172   See Word Fun answer key

page 173
1. electricity
2. power
3. energy
4. habitat
5. fuel
6. atoms
7. kinetic
8. machine
9. decibel
10. landfill
11. motor
12. horsepower
13. lightning
14. conservation
15. artificial

page 176   AWV

page 177   AWV

page 178   a chair

page 179
1. carbon, oxygen
2. carbon, hydrogen, oxygen
3. hydrogen, oxygen
4. iron, oxygen
5. hydrogen, sulfur, oxygen

page 180
Bob: 24
Alice: 120
Bill: 90
Mary: 144
Hattie: 30
Scott: 72
Luann: 21

page 184   AWV

page 186   AWV

page 187   AWV

page 189
1. atoms
2. rocks
3. solid

4. water
5. energy
6. crust
7. reflect

Circled word is *science*.

page 190   AWV

page 191   See Word Fun answer key

page 192
1. lever
2. oxygen
3. medicine
4. carbon
5. harbor
6. copper
7. matter
8. wedge
9. silver
10. liquid
11. physical
12. weight
13. diamond
14. pulley
15. aspirin
16. solid

page 194
1. arm
2. abacus
3. air
4. ache
5. acid
6. adapt
7. aerial
8. agriculture
9. airport
10. alarm
11. allergic
12. amphibian
13. anchor
14. apple
15. arithmetic
16. artery
17. ash
18. astronomy

page 195   airplane

page 196   See Word Fun answer key

page 197
1. ecology
2. geology
3. biology
4. botany
5. physics
6. medicine
7. psychology
8. zoology
9. sociology
10. astronomy

page 199
1. back
2. ball
3. balloon
4. bank

5. bark
6. bottle
7. bass
8. burn
9. bee
10. brook
11. bud
12. blood
13. bow
14. bones
15. blue
16. blackboard
17. bite
18. blade

page 200
1. rabbit
2. raccoon
3. saddle
4. freeze
5. suffocate
6. gaggle
7. jackknife
8. blood
9. alligator
10. ammunition
11. cannon
12. appliance
13. parrot
14. moss
15. battery
16. vacuum
17. nozzle

(Some answers will vary.)

page 201
1. cable
2. coffee
3. calorie
4. camera
5. concrete
6. cell
7. canoe
8. canyon
9. capillary
10. carbon dioxide
11. cardinal
12. caribou
13. cancer
14. catfish
15. carton
16. chalk
17. century
18. chest

page 202 See Word Fun answer key
page 203 cactus plant
page 204
1. dew
2. dam
3. dynamite
4. drug
5. design
6. deflate

7. daylight
8. dolphin
9. dagger
10. delta
11. darkness
12. damp
13. deer
14. degree
15. diamond
16. dusk
17. doctor
18. density

page 205 AWV
page 206 AWV
page 208
1. gun
2. gaggle
3. gait
4. gastric
5. gavel
6. geometry
7. geology
8. germ
9. gesture
10. glacier
11. glance
12. gold
13. grain
14. gravity
15. grow
16. gulp
17. gutter
18. granite

page 209
1. hypothesis
2. moon
3. erosion
4. Milky Way
5. fossils
6. 5 billion years
7. atom
8. avalanche
9. eras
10. computer age
11. iceberg
12. space shuttle

page 210
1. habitat
2. halo
3. horse
4. hamster
5. hawk
6. herd
7. health
8. heart
9. helicopter
10. helium
11. hen
12. hibernate
13. hickory
14. hoof

15. heredity
16. hart
17. hatchet

page 211
1. lung
2. orbit
3. generator
4. solid
5. tricycle
6. bicycle
7. tree
8. iron
9. chalk
10. wrench
11. turtle
12. table
13. iron
14. wood
15. vulture
16. lion
17. record
18. nylon
19. steps
20. time

page 214
1. light
2. labor
3. lamb
4. latitude
5. lava
6. lash
7. leopard
8. lift
9. lightning
10. liquid
11. living
12. limb
13. lumber
14. longitude
15. loose
16. lion
17. lighthouse
18. lasso

page 215
tree

page 216
1. mallet
2. microscope
3. malaria
4. mammal
5. mariner
6. machine
7. muzzle
8. magnet
9. marine
10. musket
11. machete
12. mane
13. motor
14. mirror
15. moose
16. motion

17. mold
18. monkey
19. Mercury
20. Mars

page 217
top: AWV

bottom:
a. hair dryer
b. toaster
c. power saw
d. clothes dryer
e. can opener

page 218
1. crow
2. snake
3. pig
4. horse
5. puppy
6. lion
7. duck
8. elephant
9. bird
10. wolf
11. owl
12. sheep
13. bee
14. turkey
15. frog
16. cat
17. bull
18. cat
19. mouse
20. dog

page 219
1. pace
2. paddle
3. paint
4. palm
5. pill
6. photograph
7. pilot
8. pine
9. pipe
10. piston
11. plasma
12. poison
13. pond
14. porpoise
15. print
16. pulse
17. python

page 220
top:
1. plums
2. cherries
3. peaches
4. apples
5. grapes
6. oranges
7. bananas
8. pineapple
9. pears

10. apricots

bottom:
1. peanut
2. almond
3. hazel
4. Brazil
5. cashew
6. walnut
7. pecan
8. pistachio

page 221   See Word Fun answer key

page 222   AWV

page 223   1. rabbit
2. radio
3. raft
4. railroad
5. ramp
6. rasp
7. ray
8. record
9. reflect
10. reindeer
11. reservoir
12. reverse
13. rice
14. rock
15. rocket
16. revolve
17. ruby
18. rust

page 224   1. k
2. h
3. i
4. l
5. c
6. f
7. e
8. a
9. j
10. d
11. g
12. b

page 225   1. safety
2. saliva
3. salmon
4. sun
5. sand
6. Saturn
7. saw
8. scales
9. scavenger
10. science
11. scissors
12. scale
13. screw
14. scalp
15. sea

16. sediment
17. shears
18. shell

page 226   1. seal
2. maple
3. star
4. steel
5. marble
6. palm
7. earth
8. siren
9. time
10. tea
11. spider
12. wasp
13. peach
14. disease
15. wolf
16. horse
17. rifle
18. mane

page 227   1. arm
2. den
3. owl
4. inches
5. boa
6. can
7. crow
8. pear
9. fur
10. ant
11. itch
12. oak
13. corn
14. pen
15. rice
16. ape
17. eel
18. ear

page 228   1. tail
2. tame
3. taste
4. tear
5. telephone
6. telescope
7. television
8. tendons
9. theory
10. thermometer
11. thread
12. tie
13. time
14. tire
15. TNT
16. toe
17. tricycle

page 229   1. water
2. path

3. CO_2
4. reptile
5. movement
6. sphere
7. igneous rock
8. gasoline
9. volume measure
10. gas
11. measured by degrees
12. mile
13. Uranus
14. definite shape
15. inclined plane
16. H_2O
17. sound waves
18. mollusk
19. 0 degree freeze
20. frog

page 230
1. water
2. dry
3. mountain
4. kinetic energy
5. astronomy
6. fish
7. moon or planet
8. wastefulness
9. natural
10. gas
11. humid
12. solid
13. mountain
14. hill
15. river
16. rubber
17. manpower
18. quiet
19. foot
20. ankle

page 231 AWV

page 233
1. whale
2. wind
3. wolf
4. whistle
5. wax
6. wire
7. well
8. wool
9. weight
10. winch
11. wedge
12. wrist
13. west
14. wet
15. winter
16. war
17. wheel
18. weather

page 234 AWV

page 235 AWV

page 238
1. vertebrates
2. rudder
3. ivory
4. an air bladder
5. an amphibian
6. hibernate
7. backbones
8. pearl
9. plankton
10. owl/hawk
11. gills
12. arteries
13. saliva
14. cannot
15. a reflex
16. trachea
17. clean
18. cranium

page 239
1. mollusk
2. cirrus
3. air
4. water
5. tusks
6. to prey on another
7. an antenna
8. shell and food
9. foe
10. eye
11. heart
12. bile
13. an involuntary
14. bicep
15. marrow
16. changes in size
17. stomach
18. anemometer

page 240
1. multiple
2. hemispheres
3. optic
4. lens
5. troposphere
6. wind vane
7. knot
8. hydro
9. humid
10. velocity
11. Saturn
12. astronomy
13. light
14. a meteor
15. pedometer
16. calorie
17. temperature
18. geology

page 241
1. conservation
2. energy
3. fuel

4. kinetic
5. machines
6. habitat
7. erosion
8. wind
9. dump
10. artificial
11. vacuum
12. ultrasonic
13. machine
14. gas
15. carbon dioxide
16. simple machine
17. weight
18. an ache

page 242
1. F
2. T
3. T
4. F
5. T
6. F
7. F
8. T
9. T
10. F
11. F
12. T
13. F
14. T
15. T
16. T
17. F
18. F

page 243
1. F
2. F
3. T
4. T
5. F
6. F
7. T
8. T
9. F
10. F
11. T
12. T
13. F
14. T
15. T
16. T
17. T
18. T

page 244
1. T
2. T
3. T
4. F
5. T
6. T
7. T
8. F
9. F

10. F
11. F
12. F
13. F
14. T
15. T
16. T
17. F
18. F

page 245
1. F
2. T
3. F
4. F
5. T
6. F
7. F
8. T
9. T
10. T
11. T
12. T
13. F
14. T
15. T
16. F
17. T
18. F

page 246
1. astronomy
2. turtle
3. motor
4. ankle
5. ocean
6. marrow
7. bone
8. epidermis
9. eel
10. lung
11. pearl
12. copperhead
13. meteor
14. snake
15. hair

page 247
1. plant
2. duststorm
3. bicycle
4. sewing
5. evaporation
6. contaminate
7. copper
8. bench
9. orbit
10. heat
11. limestone
12. steamship
13. force
14. hybrid
15. balloon
16. digest

page 248

1. 18
2. 3
3. 6
4. 12
5. 16
6. 7
7. 15
8. 1
9. 10
10. 11
11. 20
12. 13
13. 5
14. 4
15. 9
16. 19
17. 14
18. 8
19. 2
20. 17

page 249

1. 11
2. 9
3. 15
4. 10
5. 6
6. 12
7. 17
8. 2
9. 18
10. 4
11. 13
12. 8
13. 3
14. 19
15. 14
16. 20
17. 16
18. 7
19. 1
20. 5

page 250

1. 1
2. 3
3. 18
4. 10
5. 11
6. 19
7. 17
8. 20
9. 12
10. 8
11. 4
12. 7
13. 9
14. 13
15. 15
16. 14
17. 16
18. 5
19. 2
20. 6

page 251

1. 15
2. 13
3. 11
4. 12
5. 14
6. 1
7. 4
8. 3
9. 5
10. 2
11. 7
12. 8
13. 10
14. 9
15. 6
16. 18
17. 19
18. 17
19. 16
20. 20

WORD FUN ANSWER KEY

page 44

page 66

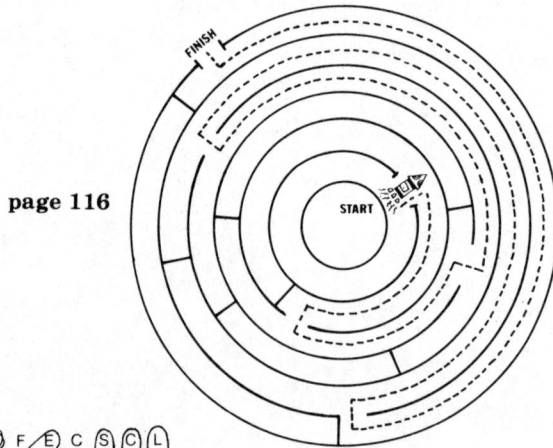

page 116

page 82

page 104

page 124

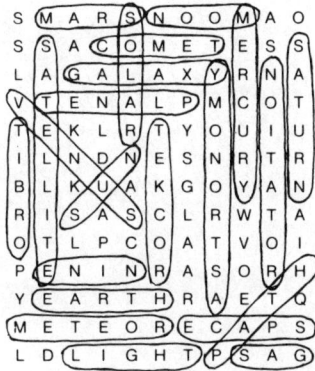

page 144

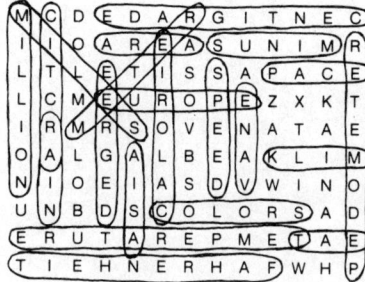

page 164

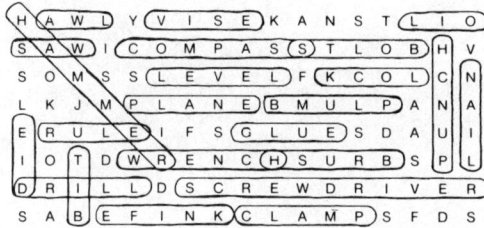

page 172

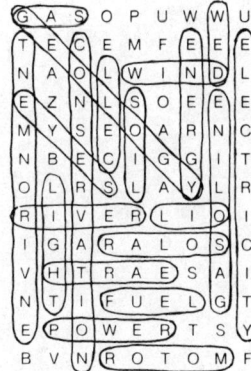

page 196

```
U W I T H N G S L C A Z
C O P P E R G O L D E B
H R I U T C R E A M E R O
A A N R G H A F T R I W
R N K P P T N U Z Y O N
T G B L U E A S T E U N
R E D E K G T C D L Q A
E E B O R H R I M L R P
U N B P G L A A H O U W
S I L V E R M K Y W T L
E W A Z F U E Q I B T D
R G C L P S T E L O I V
T M K N B T A T N C O E
```

page 191

```
A E L S D R I T R A C Y
S X A I W E R C S A H E
J A L I O V W E D G E N I
P O G X R E T T A M M I C
S Y M B O L Q N O R I C
M D O O W E G N A H C I D
E L M A C H I N E S A D E
G T G O L D I U Q I L M
B L A C I S Y H P O O M
A P U L L E Y E N A L P
L A I R E T A M B L U E
```

page 202

```
L T J H I M A L A Y A N
E I B A S D E K Y S X N
O G O F G S A B H E N R
P E B N E U B P L D A C
A R C M I A A E E E L O
R P A N T H E R S X C R
D I T T A F B S M I N X
S T R I P E D I L M A C
L I N U R K C A L B M X
K J S U P I C N A L U N Y
B S P O T T E D K M P Y
Y T T I K T O L E C O L
```

page 221

```
T G D M O R T A R B A Y S
A A A U A S S F L I N T E
T L G S P A W Z Z U B C R
A I G K B G W O L B A U O
S E E O R S O R E Y T C
H N R T N A D R W D O L K
W G M A C E A O O A N E E
O N I M P T B E N N S T
R E W R S K N I F E W S A
R L O T S I P B E R W S O
A T E N O N N A C G T O W
```

INDEX